Gavin Carlyle

Moses and the Prophets

Gavin Carlyle

Moses and the Prophets

ISBN/EAN: 9783742809834

Manufactured in Europe, USA, Canada, Australia, Japa

Cover: Foto ©Lupo / pixelio.de

Manufactured and distributed by brebook publishing software (www.brebook.com)

Gavin Carlyle

Moses and the Prophets

MOSES AND THE PROPHETS;

*THEIR UNSHAKEN TESTIMONY
AS AGAINST THE 'HIGHER CRITICISM' BASED
ON NATURALISM.*

REV. GAVIN CARLYLE, M.A.

LONDON:
ELLIOT STOCK, 62, PATERNOSTER ROW, E.C.
1890.

PREFACE.

THERE can be no dispute as to the value of genuine criticism, and as to its great services in recent times. Much light has been thrown by it, on both the Old and New Testaments, in our own day. The increase of knowledge in all directions, which is a most marked feature of our age, has given new interest to many portions of the Scriptures. Even the assaults of opponents have resulted in advantage in this respect, as when Neander wrote his 'Life of Christ' in answer to Strauss's book, and Archdeacon Farrar, Dr. Geikie, and the late Dr. Edersheim made researches and gave new vividness to the minute events of our Lord's history, in consequence partly of the book of Rénan and others of similar spirit. Healthy criticism has done much in our days to vivify both the Old and New Testaments. More attention is now paid than formerly to the characteristics of the various writers, and to the special circumstances under which they wrote; while we have much greater knowledge of the countries and of the manners and customs of the people. Genuine criticism, with its wide researches and investigations, is invaluable.

But there is a so-called criticism with which the term

'higher criticism' has become generally associated, which is of a very different influence. There are many writers and critics, especially in Germany, who proceed on the understanding that *no cognizance* even is to be taken of revelation or miracle or prophecy. Everything in the Old Testament and in the New is to be accounted for on natural principles. The alleged miracles were ordinary events magnified intentionally or by tradition, or invented for a purpose. The alleged prophecies were shrewd guesses in a few instances, but generally vague records of events that had happened, put into the form of prophecy, and then imputed falsely to some old writer. There was no revelation, for the idea of a living God ruling the earth and communicating with men is a mere subjective idea evolved by the prophets in the later period. The whole Scriptures are to be tested and accounted for on the principles of naturalism. Whatever the philosophy—Hegelianism, Agnosticism, Materialism, Darwinism—or whether there be no professed philosophy at all, those critics we refer to agree in this, that the standpoint of critical inquiry into the Old and New Testaments must be naturalistic—that is, that the truth or otherwise of the narratives must be tested by their being in accordance with the possibilities of ordinary everyday life, that miracles and prophecy and Divine revelation or manifestation of any kind must be ignored or put out of account. We use the wide embracing terms 'naturalism,' 'naturalistic,' because there has been an attempt to mislead, by asserting that such and such leading critics do not deny the possibility of miracles. This is true of some who do not profess to philosophize, but who still *rigidly* and *avowedly* apply the naturalistic test.

Graf, Kuenen, and Wellhausen, for instance, recognised leaders in 'the higher criticism' of the Old Testament, have applied naturalism as an indisputable test. They profess to account for the Old Testament as a record of ordinary human events. All that is extraordinary, viz., miraculous or prophetic or professed revelation, must be explained away. We may note also that they do not believe in the wondrous events that lie at the basis of Christianity—as the Incarnation and the Resurrection. Their principles of criticism apply equally to the New as to the Old Testament miracles. Pfleiderer and others, in treating of the New Testament, use exactly the same methods as those mentioned in dealing with the Old. It is perfectly foolish to say that we can, on the principles of this 'higher criticism,' give up the Old Testament and retain the New, or even its central facts. Kuenen, in the beginning of his 'History of Israel,' states distinctly as his standpoint, that he puts aside all idea of revelation or miracle, and weighs everything by the merely human and natural possibilities.

This method of inquiry, with a foregone conclusion of the most sweeping import, by which the non-reality of revelation and miracle is taken for granted, must not only change but revolutionize, the Scripture history and literature. The Divine and miraculous, including prophetic, are so interwoven with the Scriptures — as the web and woof — that any attempt to get rid of them must involve enormous changes. The history as it stands, for the most part, reads quite naturally and easily as a true history, if Israel were indeed chosen, and also directed and guided, by God, from the beginning. But if not—if there were no Divine guidance and no signs and wonders, the growth of the wondrous literature must be accounted for—and the narratives of great miracles must have been written many centuries after the events they profess to describe are alleged to have occurred; the elaborate code of laws must have been introduced at a later period in the history of the nation, when it had had time to advance in civilization; the lofty poetry of the Psalms must have been the product of an age succeeding centuries of culture. It is easily seen how the whole of this criticism hangs together, and how all depends on the granting of the premises.

But are these premises to be granted? And are there not insuperable difficulties on the other side? Have men any right to *take for granted* that there was no direct revelation or special providence of God, and no miracles or prophecy? The evidences, for instance, of many prophecies being true predictions are overwhelming.

We can well understand the position of the acknowledged heads of the school of Old Testament 'higher criticism.' They have, like Baur, made a tremendous effort to make good an untenable position, that of treating the sacred history apart from a Divine Being and special Divine action.

But we cannot by any means understand the position of many in this country who accept the results and deny the premises—who, for instance, acknowledge the inspiration of the Scriptures, and yet adopt theories which involve, in the preparation of the books, every kind of deception. There is something most mysterious in their position which requires explanation. They even tell us of the great comfort they have derived from theories which charge the writers of many portions of the Old Testament, as Hilkiah and Ezra, with literary frauds of the basest type. They ought to enlighten us a little more as to the means by which they get such comfort. They might, as far as we can understand, just as intelligently say that Strauss's or Baur's or Pfleiderer's criticisms of the Gospels and explaining away of the Resurrection gave them much consolation. We are not afraid of the influence of the naturalists when they appear candidly as such, but we dread a kind of insidious Jesuitical influence from those who profess to maintain contradictories. The very representations they give of the acts of men, always reputed as holy, and attested as such by their writings, are fitted to destroy reverence and to undermine truth. There is not the smallest indication in their history that the ancient Jews considered, as many assert, 'pious frauds' to be lawful—that they had loose ideas on this subject. The indications of history are that they were most particular in guarding authorship; and the writings themselves everywhere attest that the writers regarded lying and fraud of every kind as the very basest of vices.

We seek to point out the *indissoluble* connection between the naturalistic basis and the revolutionary results of the 'higher criticism'—to show, further, the moral and other impossibilities in the way of such results being true, and to exhibit how these results, if accepted, undermine the authority of our Lord and His Apostles, who built up the Church on the Scriptures, as testifying of the Christ and shadowing forth His person and His kingdom. If we deny or ignore a personal God and the supernatural, there is no need of critical inquiry at all. We may, without further discussion, give up the Scriptures and give up Christianity.

There is practically much danger. The faith of numbers has been rudely shaken. The callous and careless are encouraged. The pulpits in very many places are giving forth an uncertain sound. Scepticism raises its head in triumph. We have such tales as 'Robert Elsmere' read eagerly by the millions, in which the statements of this sweeping criticism are assumed as proved, and those who adhere to it are regarded as intellectual giants. Many, like Robert Elsmere, whose honesty we admire, though we do not respect his intelligence, are driven almost to despair. It is no wonder that pessimism makes such advances. Goethe, the greatest poet or genius of the century, who was permeated with the sceptical spirit, said to Eckermann: 'People have always considered me as a spoiled child of fortune. It is true I have not had anything to complain of; and yet my life has been only a tissue of pains and chagrins, and out of seventy-five years I cannot count four weeks of pure enjoyment.' How many a humble Christian with strong faith in the word of God and no genius has had a continual happiness for many years, even in the midst of buffetings and trials!

It is most important to spiritual life, and also to the awakening of the careless, that the faith be held clearly and distinctly. Haziness in religion seems to be greatly admired by many at present. But what is always the result of haziness in business?—bankruptcy and ruin; or of haziness in knowledge and science?—utter confusion; or of haziness in government?—anarchy. In religion we must have a clear and distinct faith. There are great mysteries, but we must know what the mysteries are, and have an intelligent reason for holding them. Religion centres in love; but we must know of God and of His love to us—and especially of redeeming love—before the affections of the heart can be drawn out towards Him. The source of such knowledge is in the Scriptures, regarded as the message of God, and realized to us personally by the indwelling of the Spirit. Low views of the authority of the Scriptures must, therefore, undermine religion and the Churches—as has been amply proved in recent times in Germany, Switzerland, and Holland.

The 'higher criticism' as applied to the Old Testament may be said to have culminated in Professor Kuenen's 'Hexateuch,' a book of remarkable ability of its kind. In it he brings together the whole results which he thinks have been attained. We may state them briefly. There was nothing of the Old Testament till the beginning of the prophetic period—eight or nine centuries before Christ. 'The chief consideration that forbids us to assign a higher antiquity is based on the contents. The sagas about the patriarchs, the exodus, and the conquest, presuppose the unity of the people (which only came into existence with and by means of the monarchy) as a long-accomplished fact, which had come to dominate the whole conception of the past completely.' The first document written was the Yahwistic or Jehovistic document, in the North Israelite kingdom, within the ninth or quite at the beginning of the eighth century B.C. This document is referred to as J. The Elohistic document—referred to as E—came next, about 750 B.C. Both were expanded and recast in the second half of the seventh century B.C. At some period later than 650 B.C. these documents (J and E) were supplemented and worked over as a whole. It does not appear that the writer of Deuteronomy (referred to as D), which was written by Hilkiah, had J and E before him as a whole. The Sinaitic legislation in these early documents (J and E) embraced nothing but the decalogue. Then there are two priestly documents, composed by priests and in the priestly interest. The first, referred to as P^1, appeared near the close of the Babylonish captivity. The second priestly document, referred to as P^2, was post-exilian. It begins with the creation of heaven and earth, and passes on, after a rapid survey of the history of the primitive world and the patriarchs, to the narrative of Israel's release from Egypt and the legislation of Moses, and ends with the settlement of Israel in Canaan. The reason for assigning it these important elements is thus given: 'Not till the period we have named could any system of legislation treat the people as a religious community or congregation rather than as an independent body politic; assign the foremost place to the high priest; make the centralization of worship, as an accomplished fact, its point of departure; explain the difference between priests and Levites genealogically, and enforce it with utmost rigour; make such provision as we find in P^2 for the support of priests and Levites alike; and, finally, regulate the whole worship after the pattern observed in these laws.' The date of this second priestly document (P^2) was within the sixth or the first half of the fifth century B.C. He now notes that it is not merely the priestly legislation that appears in P^2, but its historical framework. 'It is incorrect to assert that the date we have arrived at for the laws is inapplicable to the priestly narrative. Not only the historical sections of P^2 in Exodus, Numbers, and Joshua, but those sections in Genesis i. to Exodus vi. which belong to P^2 are post-exilian.' The priestly author builds upon

J and E, but alters freely to suit his purposes. The whole was revised and put together in its present form by an editor at a later period.

Such is a brief outline of the results of the 'higher criticism' as completed, and we have reason to be glad that Professor Kuenen has so clearly defined it, because we know what we are dealing with, whereas mere vague statements cannot be grappled with. We see here that it is not only the priestly legislation but the historical framework which is post-exilian. In these lectures we have shown how, if this test be applied, the whole theory is exploded. The difficulties also of introducing after the exile a whole system of priests and Levites, with forged genealogies, as an innovation among those who had surely some traditions of a not distant past, must have been insuperable. And where possibly could the materials have been got for inventing the grand history of creation, as given in Genesis i., in the post-exilian period. And remember that it was after this P^2 that the great mass of the Psalms and of the prophetic supposed interpolations had to be written. How was the great outburst of Jewish post-exilian genius not recorded? or why should the authors have wished to impute all done by themselves to past ages?

Professor Kuenen, who has the merit of being clear, defines in his 'Prophets and Prophecy of Israel' very distinctly the position of himself and the Old Testament 'higher critics' to the New Testament: 'It is the common conviction of all the writers of the New Testament that the Old Testament is inspired by God, and is thus invested with Divine authority. The remark made, as it were, in a passage of the fourth gospel, that "the Scripture cannot be broken," is assented to by all the writers without distinction. In accordance with this they ascribe Divine foreknowledge to the Israelitish prophets. And far, indeed, from limiting this foreknowledge to generalities, and thus depriving it of all its importance, they refer us repeatedly to the agreement between specific prophetical utterances and single historical facts, and have no hesitation in declaring their convictions, both that the prophet spoke of these specific facts, and that they, under God's direction, occurred, 'in order that the word of the prophet might be fulfilled. . . .' 'Its' (the New Testament) 'judgment concerning the origin and nature of the prophetical expectations and concerning their relations to the historical reality may be regarded as *diametrically opposed* to ours.'

It is interesting to notice in contrast that the greatest perhaps of genuine critics (Niebuhr) wrote as follows :

'In my opinion he is not a Protestant Christian who does not receive the historical facts of Christ's earthly life in their literal acceptation, with all their miracles, as equally authentic with any event recorded in history. . . . A Christianity after the fashion of the modern philosophers and pantheists, without a personal God, without immortality, without human individuality, without historic faith, is no Christianity at all to me. I have often said that I do not know what to do with a metaphysical God, and that I will have none but the God of the Bible, who is heart to heart with us.'

The Reverend Dr. Stanley Leathes, Professor of Hebrew in King's College, London, has kindly sent at my request a note for publication in this volume. It is as follows:

'It is a mistake to suppose that the traditional view of the Old Testament as an historical record of the revelation of the Divine will must vanish before an increased critical knowledge of Hebrew. Nothing can be more untrue, though we are frequently bidden to believe this upon high authority.

'The fact is, there are two ways of studying the records of the Old Testament: one is in a believing spirit, and the other is in a sceptical spirit. It is possible to study the most unimpeachable history—that, for instance, of Thucydides—sceptically.

'The real question is : Are we willing to concede miracle and prophecy in the Old Testament, or not? If we are not, then we must begin by rejecting the Gospels and the Acts. If we are honestly willing to accept these narratives as *bonâ-fide* narratives of fact, then I am bold to say that the profoundest knowledge of Hebrew and its cognate languages will discover to us nothing that will make it more difficult to recognise the like phenomena in the history and literature of the Old Testament.'

I have had also by request the following note from the Reverend Dr. Adolph Saphir, so well-known and highly esteemed, and a Hebrew of the Hebrews :

'The modern hypothesis, which regards the Pentateuch not as the work of Moses, but the production of unknown authors in the time of Ezra and subsequent periods, is brought forward with so much erudition, ingenuity, and confidence, that many minds are disturbed and confused, especially as the vital principles and important results of the new theory are more or less kept in the background. It is natural that a profound knowledge of Hebrew and cognate languages should be regarded as an element of great importance in this inquiry. But when Hebrew scholars of equal eminence can attribute the same sections of Genesis to the period before Moses and to the period after the exile—thus differing to the utmost possible extent—it is evident that Hebrew scholarship by itself cannot furnish cogent arguments in this inquiry.

These Lectures were delivered in connection with the Glasgow Working Men's and West of Scotland Sabbath Protection Association, in August last. At the close of the course, it was moved by the Rev. Dr. Kerr, and unanimously agreed to, that the lecturer be requested to publish them.

G. C.

CONTENTS.

LECTURE I.
PAGE

Criticism true and false — Naturalism the basis of the false — Applied to the New Testament as well as the Old — The present centre of the battle, the Old Testament — Attempt to take the Old Testament to pieces — The books cut into fragments — Insuperable difficulties not considered — Literary and moral impossibilities — Testimony of tradition — Josephus — The whole a desperate connected effort to reconcile the existence of the Old Testament with naturalism — Statement of Henry Rogers as to the Pentateuch - . . . . 1—20

LECTURE II.

The attacks on special books — Genesis — The account of Creation — The patriarchal histories — Internal evidence of their truthfulness — The accuracy of the narratives of Exodus established strikingly by recent observations and discoveries in Egypt and the desert — Not only a priestly code, but many alleged *facts*, connected with the existence of the priesthood and sacrifice, interwoven with the attested history — Dr. Lansing's testimony to the accuracy of Exodus as to Egypt — The late incorporation of the priestly facts inexplicable — If it fail here, the whole of the so-called 'higher criticism' breaks down — This the crucial point — Deuteronomy's own witness to the period and method of its preparation — All the scenes vividly presented — Moses seen and heard — Evidences of truthfulness in the narrative of David especially in the thorough exposure of his great sin — The Psalms — No reason at all for upsetting the ideas of time and authorship, except the connected system of the naturalists granted — The Prophets — The spirit of all their writings — Denunciation of fraud — Yet supposed to be engaged in the basest frauds — The style of each prophet discernible — The Dean of Canterbury's testimony — The fierce attack on Daniel — Dr. Pusey's vindication — Its position unshaken — Why so bitterly assailed . . . 21—43

LECTURE III.

The historic position as to the Scriptures — The Jewish Church — The Apostles — The human characteristics and surroundings of the writers clearly apparent as in any other writings — But the Divine direction and unity also apparent — Unity of teaching from Genesis to Revelation — as to God — as to man — as to evil agents — Universal characteristics — brevity with marvellous fulness in all the histories both of Old and New Testaments—contrast of Jewish traditions and spurious Gospels—undeniable fulfilled predictions—their imaging of Christ before He appeared—The whole Scripture inspired—This the position of the Jewish Church—Accepted by our Lord and testified to by Him with all clearness—He did not conform to the prejudices of the age—He opposed the false teaching as to tradition and ecclesiasticism, but maintained the absolute authority of Scripture —The blasphemy of supposing Jesus mistaken—The Apostles built up the Church on the Old Testament as the word of God —The Messianic prophecies—Kuenen's unfounded statement as to 'pious frauds'—The Old and New Testaments bound together as a living organism—Weak concessions of those ignorant of the drift of the controversy—The battle really against all supernatural religion—The alleged opposition of science unfounded—The argument for God from design still as clear as ever—The presumption that all miracles are to be set aside as not true an unintelligent assumption—Evolution as a philosophy of the universe not even made likely—If it were, it would not necessarily destroy miracles - 44—74

LECTURE IV.

The practical effect of this so-called 'higher criticism'—Desolation of Christianity—Cuts down all miracles, including that of the Resurrection—Deadening influence on religion and Churches —Proved in Germany, Switzerland and Holland—Influence among ourselves—It leads either to materialism or superstition —Cardinal Newman and the Church of Rome—The struggle one of vital moment—Reading and preaching of the Scriptures as the word of God the only means of reviving the Church at the Reformation and in every age—In the Scriptures we behold Christ—And through them, under the Spirit's influence, we grow into His image—The present a battle for the very existence of Christianity—The result not doubtful - 75—86

CONCLUSION . . . . . . 87—90

APPENDIX A.

The poet Burns, by a higher critic of a future century - 91—98

APPENDIX B.

What the Scriptures would have been had the miracles been invented by men, as seen in Jewish Talmud and spurious Gospels - · · · · · 99—102

APPENDIX C.

The Dean of Canterbury (Dr. Payne Smith) on the absurdities of the 'higher critics,' and the marked styles of the different prophets · · · · · · 102—104

MOSES AND THE PROPHETS.

LECTURE I.

THE HIGHER CRITICISM: ITS BASIS.

THERE are *two* kinds of professed criticism, which are essentially distinct in their methods. A criticism founded on historic investigation, or satisfactory linguistic evidence, all *must* accept—so far as its facts are established. Everything that tends to throw light upon the place and time at which books were written, and the surrounding circumstances, is of value. Much interest has been added to the Scriptures in our own days by the increased information of all kinds now accessible. We can realize much more clearly than formerly the circumstances under which many of the writers wrote. The events of the Gospels, for instance, are more real and more impressive, as we now understand better the whole surroundings.

But there is a criticism of *another kind*, which is *entirely different*, which *must be separated altogether from it*. This criticism is based on a foregone conclusion. Many Biblical critics, especially in Germany, deny that there is a living personal God; or if Agnostics that, if there is, He can possibly make Himself known. They therefore proceed in their criticisms on the HUGE *assumption* that all references to the sayings or doings of God in the Old and New Testaments are imaginations, or hallucinations, or designed deceptions; all professed miracles and prophecies are untrue; all representations of God's intercourse with men are imaginary; all asserted messages from God are either self-delusions on the part of the writers, or 'pious,' as they are termed—really impious—frauds. We have no hesitation in saying that a large proportion of the professed critical results which have excited alarm in recent times is based on these *tremendous assumptions*. The criticisms referred to treat the Scriptures as, without question, the product of mere human genius; they regard all references to a living God communicating with men in any way as inventions; they deal with professed miracles and prophecies as delusions or lies; and they attempt to account for the narratives of them on naturalistic principles. Such criticism of books which are full professedly of the actions of a personal God, and of the supernatural, *must*, logically, lead to a change of all former ideas in regard to them. But what we have to urge, and what is forgotten and perhaps often unknown, is, that this revolutionary criticism at present in vogue is based on such assumptions; and that if these assumptions are without reason, as we believe them to be, it has, except in a few small details, no *value*.

The well-known Baur, of Tübingen, was a man of vast erudition and great shrewdness—the trainer of David Strauss. His aim was to account for the origin of the New Testament on purely natural principles—that is, on the basis of its being a merely human production—anything supernatural being impossible. Its account of Christ's wondrous birth, miracles, resurrection, ascension, etc., and of the extraordinary powers of the early Church, were necessarily fables. How, then, did these books originate? He set himself with great learning, and acuteness, and ingenuity, and high intellectual power, to account for them. He was a man of great sagacity, whose countenance cannot be forgotten by those who have seen him, as I did. The result is well known, and may be thus generally stated: Paul was really the founder of Christianity. His fervid imagination led him to believe in an extraordinary vision of Jesus. *He* gave that impulse to the new Jewish sect which made it of world-wide importance. Four of his Epistles laid the basis. There arose gradually around them the Gospel narratives and other books. A great conflict between the Petrine and Pauline schools accounted for the special characteristics of many of the writings of the New Testament. Jesus being the centre of the new religion, there grew up around His person the wondrous events recorded of Him. In a century or two, when the conflicts had passed away, books were collected and recognised as the authoritative books of Christianity.

This system of Baur, by which he attempted with rare ingenuity and intellectual power to account for the inspired writings of the New Testament on purely natural principles, has broken down at all points. There are abundant historic evidences that the books—not only those four Epistles of Paul, but his other Epistles and all the Gospels—belong to the first century, and appeared in an age when there must have been still many eye and ear witnesses of the professed miracles. Professor Charteris has, in his

'Canonicity' and in his 'Croall Lectures,' collected perfectly conclusive evidence on this subject. A master-mind has done his very best to account for Christianity apart from revelation and miracles, and has failed. Thus, indirect evidence is given of the impossibility of accounting for Christianity apart from God and the supernatural. The position is seen to be all the stronger after the futile attack. But though Baur's ingeniously-constructed fabric has fallen to pieces, the attacks on the New Testament have not ceased. Professor Pfleiderer, of Berlin, represents numbers of German theologians who still deny the supernatural mission of Jesus, and who try to account for the New Testament—its description of the origin and person of Christ and its miracles—on natural principles. The most able and intelligent of the attacks has been defeated; but there are many who are so inveterately bound to naturalism that nothing will convince them. They still cling to childish explanations of the resurrection, as well as of the miracles generally of our Lord and His Apostles.

In a pamphlet on 'The Methods of the Higher Criticism,'* by Professor Dickson, of Glasgow University, recently published, he shows how Dr. Pfleiderer, in his 'Urchristenthum,' deals with the question of the resurrection. At the close of a searching analysis, which reveals the unbounded liberties that Dr. Pfleiderer takes with books and professed recorded facts, he says: 'We have thus passed in review the details of the singular process by which the history of the resurrection, upon which the Church has built its faith in a "Risen

---

* 'The Methods of the "Higher Criticism" illustrated in an Examination of Dr. Pfleiderer's Theory as to the Resurrection,' by William Dickson, D.D. LL.D., Professor of Divinity, University of Glasgow.

Lord," is "remodelled" in the light of the latest philosophic criticism, and reduced ultimately to a visionary experience on the part of Peter. The scene and the character of the great event are wholly changed; the alleged appearances at Jerusalem are blotted out as legendary accretions; the faith of the Church is made to rest, not on the testimony of witnesses to what they had seen as objective and real, but on a psychological process in the mind of Peter, which presented its subjective results to him in the form of a vision, and impressed him with a conviction of their truth. We have seen by what an unprecedented combination of arbitrary processes —of omission, addition, substitution, inversion, transposition, invention of hypotheses, suggestion of motives, assumption of tendencies, and free play throughout of speculative imagination, transforming at pleasure the historically presented *data* into shapes that may suit the postulates of a philosophical theory—the so-called result is reached. Under such a method of procedure there are no limits to conjecture and caprice; and the "higher" critic, who wields his weapons at will, may make anything out of anything.' He concludes thus: 'The illustration which I have thus ventured to give of the working of "higher" criticism, in its most crucial application by one of its most eminent exponents, may perhaps at least suffice to show that the certainty, which in the judgment of some belongs to its results, can hardly be equally, or indeed at all, affirmed of the process by which they are reached.'

It may be noted that the attempt—now that Baur's attack has been disposed of—is to criticize the Gospel records, treating the writers as if they wrote uncertainly. It is strange that Pfleiderer, who denies the resurrection and all miracles, has been commended, and followed in details, by many belonging to professed orthodox Churches in this country.

Still, the centre of the battle is now not around the New, but around the Old Testament. The basis of attacks is the same. The ablest of the critics, as Graf, Kuenen, Wellhausen —those who are the central pillars of the new critical system, have been determined naturalists. Whatever the basis of their opinions, they are at one in the foregone conclusion that a known God, and miracles and prophecy, are not even to be considered, and they proceed to attempt to reconstruct the Old Testament on this understanding. They do not argue about it, but take their great assumption for granted.

It is singular that Professor Cheyne should venture to imply, in a letter to the *Guardian*, that Kuenen and Wellhausen do not start from a naturalistic basis. They may not propound a philosophy on the subject; but Kuenen, in the beginning of his ‘History of Israel,’ lays down his standpoint with perfect clearness, and Wellhausen takes naturalism for granted all through his writings.

But as the Old Testament is *bound up*, so to speak, with the *supernatural ;* as the living God is everywhere and everything from the beginning to the close; as His words and actions are constantly recorded ; as numbers of miracles are described and afterwards referred to ; as predictions, distinctly announced as such, appear again and again, occupying a great part of many books—it is evident to common-sense that it requires *revolutionary changes* as to the authorship of books, and the times at which they were written, to account for the sacred writings, on the understanding that there is no acting

God and no miracle nor prediction. It requires a vast amount of ingenuity—and this has certainly been exhibited. Narratives which fit in *perfectly naturally and easily* if there be a living God, and miracles and prophecy—as, for instance, the passage through the wilderness—cannot be explained but by the most ingenious and far-fetched theories if there is nothing supernatural. How did they arise or grow up? Many ages must be allowed for the traditions of such miracles as the passage through the Red Sea, the wilderness journey, etc., to develop, before they could be written down. Therefore the books must be of a much later period than represented. This really is the grand problem which these critics are attempting to solve. They wish to account for Judaism, with its extraordinary history, apart from God and miracle. They assert that the Jews were polytheists, as other nations, and that the idea of a personal God was developed only in the prophetic period. But the books of the Old Testament are full of the idea of God, therefore could not have been written till after this period. Therefore these books of the Old Testament were all written, even the earliest, at a comparatively late date. And as the idea of God was not developed, there could not have been the priesthood as it is described in the Pentateuch. The priesthood and the whole sacrificial system is consequently of comparatively late date. Therefore the priestly part of the Pentateuch must be the invention of a later age. Deuteronomy was written at an earlier period, in the reign of Josiah; it was the book not found, but invented, by Hilkiah. The Psalms, of course, as Professor Cheyne has laboured to show, in his recent Bampton Lecture, are all of a later period, because they refer to God and to the priests and the sacrifices. They were none of them composed by David, who lived before the one God was worshipped. The professed predictions were none of them written till after the events described, because prediction is impossible. Daniel, of course, appeared only after the period of Antiochus Epiphanes, as it describes events in his reign, or, as asserted recently, after the spread of Roman power, because it so clearly describes the Roman empire.

All this would be ingenious and valuable if the premises were true. It would indeed be wonderful if an intellectual people like the Jews could have been at any period so very easily imposed on. Books were invented, and represented as ancient, which reflected much on themselves as a nation; but they quietly accepted them as of Divine origin and absolute authority without inquiry. The prophets of Israel, men who wrote with the highest moral and spiritual aim, invented a history of the past and palmed it off as genuine—the *basest literary fraud* that can be perpetrated, and this not once, but, again and again, at successive periods. They imposed on the people as ancient, and, what is worse, as of Divine authority, a mass of writings which were inventions of their own—inventions intended to deceive.

But is this criticism? Is it not mere *dogmatism* attempting to force its foregone conclusions by indirect methods? If, indeed, these men are right in their idea that God cannot be known or revealed, and that there can be no interference with the laws of the material universe of a miraculous kind —that is, of a nature beyond our comprehension, viz., which we cannot explain or understand—for what appear miracles to us may be accomplished by God controlling certain forces by higher forces, as we constantly do ourselves; if there can be no God controlling the affairs of the world, or known to control them, which is really atheism, disguise it as they may—if they are right in their basis, then their criticism is a praiseworthy effort to solve what appears an insoluble problem. If God never appeared to men, never spoke to men or through men, never sent His Son into the world, never put into the mouths of prophets messages as to the future—if all related miracles are either myths or fabrications—if the whole idea of that which is popularly called 'the supernatural' is a delusion—if the world is ruled by material laws alone, which no Supreme Intelligence controls or overrules—then the criticism of these strange Old Testament books, which are interwoven with the supernatural throughout, may be welcomed as throwing light upon the most extraordinary literature that has appeared in the history of the world. But if, on the other hand, there be nothing certain in the basis—if Agnosticism be not proved—if it be a mere theory—if the unity of nature be not a mere material unity, but an intelligent adaptation of means to ends—if the universe have not grown up of itself—if all its varieties of creatures have not been developed out of some unknown atoms—if all this be false, and if there is a Supreme Ruler to control all—if there can be the superhuman, and the, to us, miraculous, the method of the criticism by which they would revolutionize the Old Testament is simply worthless, and the whole fabric they are attempting to rear is a building of cards which must fall to pieces. It will be found that even earlier critics of the school proceed quietly on the *assumption* that *ipso facto* the action of God is to be eliminated as invention or myth. They proceed in their reconstruction of the Old

Testament books on the idea that the supernatural is to be eliminated as invention—as fairy or hobgoblin stories are eliminated by the critics of English or Scottish history. They not only deny, *but they do not regard as worth considering*, the narratives of the communion of God with men, of the revelations to the patriarchs, of the marvellous delivery from Egypt, of the passage of the Red Sea, of the sojourn in the wilderness, of the host of Joshua advancing with Divine aid, of the giving of the Law amidst thunderings and lightnings from Sinai, of the acts of Deborah and Barak, of Jephthah, and Gideon, and Samson, of David, and Elijah, and Elisha, and Daniel, of God's speaking with the prophets, and giving to them revelations of the future—they *take for granted* that all these things are frauds or myths—not worth inquiring into as possible facts. Science, it is vaguely said, has condemned them, though science has never said one single word about them.

Thus they go on attempting to account for the origin of these narratives, interwoven with the whole method and structure of the books, by taking the books to pieces and making them a kind of patchwork—a piece put in here and a piece there, for a purpose—in some remotely later age; a passage inserted, for instance, about Abel and his sacrifice, after the Babylonian captivity, by priestly fraud, for the purpose of making it appear that the sacrificial laws existed from the beginning; then others about the sacrifices of Abraham and the patriarchs; then a whole priestly system invented and put into the mouth of an aged chief of renown called Moses; then the passage through the wilderness, described as a kind of background to the sacerdotal invention; then the history made to fit in afterwards—

all its parts freely tampered with to make way for the delusion, and to give it plausibility ; then wondrous psalms, denouncing lies in unmeasured terms, imputed falsely to a great king of renown—a mere savage warrior who gave unity to the nation, but never wrote one of them, and could not write at all ; then pretended prophecies written down in glowing prophetic language *after* the events had taken place, for the most pious, or, rather, impious, purpose of convincing the nation that men, that had never imagined them, had written them under God's direction ages before—and these prophecies denouncing lying in terms of unmeasured reprobation and of stern indignation—while those writing them were imposing the basest falsehoods on the people. They thus turn the books upside down, cut them into fragments, imagine not only two, but twenty, writers of Isaiah, explain how one piece was put in here and another there, all under false pretences to suit a purpose, which purpose it is very difficult indeed to understand. All the prophecies are *ipso facto*, when they plainly refer to events of history, professing to foretell them, written after the events to which they refer.

Such are the ignoble methods to which this so-called ' higher criticism ' is driven in order to account for the books of the Old Testament, on the theory that there is no God that can be known or revealed, and that there are no possible supernatural events or revelations. The extraordinary difficulty of doing so is shown in the strangeness of many of the suggestions made. There are first the difficulties of the history. The events described historically, which these critics pass over as worthless, fit in, in the most marvellous way, to the times and places in which they are said to have occurred. They are told in the simplest manner, not at all in the style either of myth or invention, which is always sensational and bombastic. The earlier history of the patriarchs, and Joseph, for instance, fits in remarkably to the period when the events are represented to have occurred, as shown by the most recent discoveries as to the then state of Egypt and surrounding countries. The extraordinary passage through the desert has been accurately traced from the narratives by most intelligent explorers of recent times, as the late Professor Palmer—the very position found suitable for the gathering of the vast multitude, as described, at the base of Sinai. Then there is accuracy in the references of the Books of Moses to Egypt, showing beyond doubt that the writer, whenever he wrote, had not only visited the country, but been brought up in it. Then there are plain evidences in the monuments of the knowledge of sacrifices at the time and before the time when the books of Moses were professedly written. The recent discoveries as to the Hittites point to the accuracy and truth of the early history as it appears in the Book of Judges,* etc. These critics have *nothing at all* to prove their position, or even make it probable, that the Jews were not consolidated as a nation till about the age of David. It is a mere assertion to which they are obliged to resort to give likelihood to their theory. They cannot give a single reason why David may not have been a great poet as well as a great king. It is a fact in history that one man has often written more genuine poetry than whole generations either before or after him, as Dante, and Chaucer, and Shakespeare, and Milton,

* Dr. Wright's book on the Hittites is invaluable, as indicating historic accuracy where it had been much impugned.

and Burns, in their respective countries. The psalms imputed to David have a literary affinity which points to unity of origin. Then as to the Prophets—down to the Book of Daniel, who is a special object of attack, because he prophesied so clearly—the genuineness and authenticity of which book have been vindicated unanswerably by Dr. Pusey and others—their theory is that the writings imputed to the prophets were full of paltry trickery, foretelling in sublime strains as future what had already happened, therefore plainly intending to deceive, and adopting the very basest kind of literary fraud.

There is nothing at all to sustain these views, but everything against them. Can anyone with the slightest power of judging character or literature peruse the writings of Isaiah, or Jeremiah, or Ezekiel, or Daniel, with their sublime moral aim, and imagine that those who wrote *any part* of these books were deliberate swindlers, imposing on the people as old prophecy what was history, committing the double offence of writing in the prophetic method, in order to deceive, and of palming off as ancient what was composed by themselves? It is a moral impossibility. Yet such is the criticism which these critics *are compelled by circumstances* to propound and defend in harmony with their theory that there is no possibility of God being known or revealed—or of the supernatural. They prove indirectly the falsity of the basis of criticism, quietly assumed, by the reckless shifts to which they are driven. The historic basis of the Old Testament is supported by strong evidence—evidence not shaken, but much strengthened, by recent discoveries, and there is really nothing in their attempt to overthrow it—apart from the anti-supernatural basis.

The Jewish history and psalms and prophecies have been accepted by the nation as sacred from the remotest known period. We know the opinion held in the time of our Lord, as recorded shortly after by Josephus. There were other writings—the Apocrypha—which they did not regard as on the same level. But their sacred writings they believed to be inspired of God, and they looked with deepest reverence upon them. This Josephus refers to as not a new, but as an old idea. How did these writings ever get that position in the Jewish national mind? They were anything but favourable to their national pride. We may imagine a nation receiving with enthusiasm, and supporting to the death, writings that praised in glowing language their heroic deeds or the prowess of their forefathers. But these writings described the weakness and follies of the Jewish people. They showed them in the worst light, as receiving wonderful favours and showing base ingratitude. They reproached them again and again with their cowardice and meanness. How, then, if they were imposed on them at a later age, did they not only receive them, but pay them such immense reverence? Or what could have even put it into the mind of those pretended historians who wrote them to write with such severity of their own ancestors? If they had been composing a fictitious history, as the critics suppose, would they not rather have praised the virtues of their ancestors, that the people might be stirred up to similar acts? And how, in the nature of things, could they possibly have imposed on a nation a burdensome ritual and an expensive priesthood, which it had never heard of before? And how could they have persuaded them that writings descriptive of recent events were old prophecies? And how could they have given such

THE HIGHER CRITICISM : ITS BASIS.

unity of style to the great prophets, so that the many fragments seem to be the production of one mind? Whether there were one or two Isaiahs, there were surely not twenty, for the writings bear the stamp of rarest genius, being poems of the sublimest character ever written in any language. There is a striking unity in Jeremiah, Ezekiel, Daniel, and the minor prophets, which cannot fail to impress anyone of literary discernment.

The more that this criticism is examined in its general outlines, the more untenable it appears. It is a *desperate effort* to reconcile the existence of the Old Testament, in its present form, with naturalism. We speak of it in its general outlines. We are quite aware that there are points of interest that have been elucidated by the researches of the naturalistic school. But, on the whole, there is exceedingly little of value, as judged by genuine criticism. They are on the wrong track for making discoveries. If one who regarded the world as the centre of the universe were to make observations on the heavens, these observations would lead to nothing, however careful or painstaking the explorer. And so, if men proceed to deal with a history in which the direct action of God is frequently traceable, with the idea that it is entirely human, they cannot possibly interpret or understand it.

We close this lecture with the following extract from an article on Colenso, in *Good Words*, by the well-known Henry Rogers, author of 'The Eclipse of Faith,' written many years ago. It applies well, especially in the latter portion, to the present state of the controversy :

'The problems we are called on to solve on the theory of the *unhistoric* character of the Pentateuch are far more difficult than any of those which, by packing his evidence and begging his premises, this writer urges against it. Let me briefly point out two or three only, all of which *must* be confronted as a necessary condition of coming to a true decision. How, then, shall we account for the intense, obstinate, and unanimous belief of the Jews for so many ages, and afterwards of their enemies, the Samaritans, in the historic character—nay, in the Mosaic authorship and inspiration—of the Pentateuch? A belief never troubled by a shadow of doubt or suspicion, or contradicted by one echo of opposing testimony; a belief which, as we shall see by-and-by, they were ever palpably interested in throwing off if *erroneous*, and yet which they would sooner die than surrender.

'This *fact* is in itself equally incomprehensible, if the Pentateuch be indeed unhistoric or (whatever date we fix for its composition) whether we regard the document as preceding or contemporaneous with their national life and institutions, or (as some wise critics, but all of yesterday, pretend) composed very late in their history, or even after the return from the Babylonish captivity. If the former be supposed, and these monstrous fables were from the beginning foisted on the nation as the true history of the events in which it originated, how can we account for its unanimously accepting them, and proceeding to mould the national life, law, and manners upon them? Above all, how shall we account for this people's affirming they had seen marvels, which everybody was appealed to as having *seen*, but which they knew had never been wrought, and on that egregious faith—or rather *lie*—proceeding to bend their necks to a burdensome yoke of laws and ceremonies, which, in the language of Peter, "neither they nor their fathers had been able to bear;" and then, to complete the thing, handing down through all coming ages, without one misgiving of heart, one faltering of doubt, one protesting whisper of conscience, this unanimous and stupendous lie? At the very least, how can we imagine a nation moulding its life, forming its institutions and manners, on what that whole nation knows, by the very appeal to it, to be a pure romance?

'It is these very difficulties that principally inclined our modern critics to contend for the LATE composition of the Pentateuch. But if *that* theory be adopted, we are soon led to some similar difficulties, and equally insurmountable. For if this book were really a late composition—long after the nation had a history of its own, and had got (no one can tell how) its institutions and its laws—how came the Jews unanimously to endorse books in which that history is throughout so egregiously caricatured, in which common facts are everywhere exaggerated into the most monstrous fables? Five thousand at the Exodus, as this critic supposes, are turned into six hundred thousand, and everything else in similar proportion—that is, five parts out of about six hundred may be supposed true! Above all, how came the Jews at that time of day to vouch for supernatural fictions of the most monstrous character so freely superfused over the whole book? How came the nation, at so late a period of their annals, to accept without a dissentient voice this document as their true history? How came they to be universally hoodwinked, so as not to perceive the juggle that was being passed upon them; or so universally wicked as to join without a murmur, that has ever reached their posterity, in adapting, consecrating, and handing down the cheat? Not one of them even for a moment relenting, in a momentary treason to this conspiracy of wickedness, so far as to express doubt or detestation of this prodigious and unanimous lie? How could they do it, if they would? or how would they do it, if they could? I say *lie*; for, however this writer and many modern infidels may politely endeavour to show that they by no means charge deliberate fraud on the compilers of the Pentateuch, it is utterly impossible, if the main facts of the Pentateuch have as little truth in them as this author supposes, and the miracles, *à fortiori*, no truth at all, to free either the writers of these documents, or the nation who accepted and vouched for them, from the most deliberate and enormous falsehood. But, lying or no lying, the thing itself is infinitely more incredible than that Englishmen should all accept and unanimously hand down to posterity, without a trace of any disagreement, "Ivanhoe" and "Kenilworth" as true episodes in our own history, and, what is more, get all future ages to believe it! This would be a *bagatelle* compared with the supposition of the whole Jewish nation—and even their bitter enemies, the Samaritans—receiving as no less than inspired truth these impudent contradictions of their true history, and, when first published, of their very *senses* and *consciousness* to boot! Again, how came this singular people to receive—not only as historically true, but as worthy of suffering martyrdom for, if called to it—records which, if not history, are but one long *libel* upon themselves? Would *this* make them more willing to toil to procure credit for that enduring and unanimous lie, by which alone these records could be effectually consigned to the veneration of posterity? Would not all patriotism, as well as everything else, lead them to denounce chronicles which are little else than chronicles of their shame? As well may we suppose Englishmen enamoured of the worst libels of the present New York press, adopting them as faithful—nay, inspired— portraits of our national character, and handing them down to posterity as worthy of the profoundest veneration! It may be said, perhaps, that the assumed privilege of being "the favourites of heaven," no matter how they used or abused it, might reconcile the Jews to being thus pilloried to all ages. I answer, first, that it is sadly evident that it was a *privilege*, which throughout their history the Jews were only too willing to forfeit; and, secondly, that though it might tickle national vanity to represent themselves as under God's immediate guidance, the pleasure would be more than balanced by the necessity of *also* saying that they ever spurned that guidance, and repaid the Divine beneficence with the most flagitious ingratitude and wickedness. Such traits, had these records been either fraudulent or fictitious, or anything but truth, it is certain that patriotism would have softened or obliterated before the nation would have received them. It might perhaps humour a man's vanity to tell how his father and grandfather had been prime ministers to some great monarch; but if he had to say at the same time that the one had embezzled the public property, and the other had been hanged for treason, he would be apt, I fancy, to exercise a wise silence about his pedigree. But, again, how shall we account, upon such a hypothesis as that of this pseudo-Colenso, for the inimitable marks of sincerity, truth, nature, artlessness, honesty, which everywhere abound in the Pentateuch, and which have in all ages made not only Jews, but Christians, believe it to be history, and neither fiction nor forgery? How shall we account for those "undesigned coincidences," many of which are as striking as those which Paley has so ingeniously insisted on in his *Horæ Paulinæ*, and of which Blunt has given us but a small *spicilegium* in his little work on this subject? How, above all, shall we account for the profound religious tone, the elevated morality, in these documents, which, if not history, are a contexture of the most shameless and conscious violations of truth? How came the sublime doctrines of Monotheism, and a purer and loftier moral code than the world had ever seen, to be given to the world in records, every page of which is stamped— if this theory be true—with the most enormous misrepresentations and the most extravagant fictions? How shall we account for the union of so much moral elevation and such unique hypocrisy, such pervading sense of the Divine presence and protestations of speaking by God's authority, with such abandoned and unblushing wickedness? For, I repeat, there is no medium in the nature of the thing between supposing the documents historically true and allowing that those who palmed them upon the world *as such*, and those who connived at and perpetuated the cheat, were among, not only the most stupendously gifted, but the most deliberately wicked of mankind.'

LECTURE II.

THE LEADING POSITIONS OF THE NATURALISTIC CRITICS CONSIDERED AS TO THE PENTATEUCH, AS TO THE PSALMS, AND AS TO THE PROPHETS.

IN beginning this second lecture I would refer again, in a few words, to the leading positions of this school of criticism in regard to the Jewish Scriptures. The theory and assertion is that the Jews had been polytheists, as other nations, up to the time of the prophets; that the idea of God as the one God, and the God of the universe, had been developed or evolved by the eighth-century prophets—that is, the eighth century before Christ. This, of course, undermined the whole early history—swept it clean away. The Israelites, it was represented, had been composed of different tribes, which gradually became a nation in the course of ages,* and had looked on their God, as the Moabites and others, as a tribal God long after the days of even David and Solomon. Thus the whole history in Genesis of the early world and the patriarchs, which implied the knowledge and the worship

---

* 'In short, the tribes were regarded and treated as individuals, and were transferred to the house of their common father in the same mutual relation in which they actually stood to each other.'—Kuenen's ' History of Israel.'

of the one God, was written at a late period, and was intentionally false, though founded possibly on a few very vague traditions worked up to suit a purpose. The passage of the wilderness might have some insignificant basis, but was, in the main, quite unhistorical. The miracles condemned it. The whole priestly system, with its ceremonial law, was a later development, worked up into its present form probably by Ezra. David was a barbarous chieftain, who did much to give unity to the tribes, which were gradually becoming a nation; but in his days there was no culture and no knowledge of God as the one living God. This idea was not developed till centuries later. The Psalms, *therefore*, were *not* written by David. The professed prophecies, where distinct in their predictions, were written after the events they professed to foretell, and put into the mouth of some old prophet or preacher of renown by a system of 'pious' frauds. The so-called Messianic prophecies were hallucinations, for all prediction was out of the question. Such is a general outline of the ideas of the revolutionary criticism, which varies in details in different writers, but in the main lines agrees. Such are the bold assertions by which, in accordance with their preconceived system—that there is no supernatural—the books of the Old Testament are to be tested. They must be swept down by the 'higher criticism' to this dead-level, whatever the difficulties. Anything more far-fetched and inconsequential has never been attempted in literature. It is well established that at a very early period, thousands of years before Christ, there were traces among different nations of the knowledge and worship of the one God. All the facts corroborative of the histories are ruthlessly tossed aside without examination.

The Jews are supposed to have been the weakest and most gullible of nations, ready, without question, to accept as prophetic, and as of Divine authority, forged writings which threw contempt on their ancestors and nation. The men who wrote with utter abhorrence of all lying, denouncing it as the curse of any people, and whose tone was that of highest righteousness and truthfulness, are represented as themselves engaged in concocting falsehoods, forging names and genealogies—for it is asserted that the long genealogies of Genesis were forgeries—imposing baseless authorities, inventing laws and ceremonies and passing them off as old, giving forth as prophecies written ages before, and, put into the form of prophecy, in order to deceive, records of events already past. Such are the shifts to which this so-called 'higher criticism' is forced, in accordance with the standpoint that there were no miracles and no Divine intercourse with men.

I shall now glance briefly at some of the books as they stand in order, considering the representations made in regard to them. The Book of Genesis stands alone in the Old Testament as a record of the early ages of the world. Its account of the creation is not only most sublime, but, when contrasted with heathen accounts, is seen to be entirely different. In some respects it agrees with them, as might be expected if they were handed down by tradition; but it rises infinitely above them. It is a most thrilling and sublime narrative of the preparation of the earth by God for the habitation of man,* not referring to its earlier period,

* 'If a man cannot feel the simple majesty, the unapproachable grandeur of this first chapter of Genesis, if he cannot discern God there of a truth, and take his shoes from off his feet, because the place on

except in the first verse, where God is said to have created the heavens and the earth, but describing the events that took place in its preparation for the advent of the human race. It speaks of the sun and moon and stars as they appear, and in relation to their action towards the earth. To have described scientifically the universe and all the progress of the past infinite would have made it utterly unintelligible. Man would, in fact, need the infinite intelligence of God to understand the fabric of the universe. Even now, science is but skirting the surface—picking up pebbles on the seashore. Whether the six days meant days or longer periods, they described the order of the processes by which the earth was renovated for man. They agree very much with the order as it is discerned in the rocks. All heathen records, including that of the Greeks, bring themselves into immediate and direct conflict with astronomical science, in even a ridiculous manner. Not so the narative of Genesis. And in various parts of the Old Testament there are sublime views of the heavens. Some of the references adapt themselves easily to the vastly-extended knowledge we have now of the universe. They could not be surpassed in sublimity. We might refer to the last chapters of Job, the 8th Psalm, the 19th Psalm, the 40th of Isaiah, and many other passages. The record in the first chapter of Genesis is most heart-

---

which he stands is holy ground—no amount of theories of reconciliation will ever convince him of its divinity. On the other hand, a broad, general correspondence between the record in Genesis and the results of scientific investigation there assuredly is.'—Dean Perowne in *Expositor* for October. He adds that Haeckel, the extreme German materialist, says that, 'From Moses, who was born about 1480 B.C., to Linnæus, who was born 1707 A.D., there has been no history of creation to be compared with it.'

stirring and beautiful, giving the sublimest ideas of the renewal of the earth for man, and culminating in his creation. It is not science, but it does not clash with science. And there was evidently a mysterious controlling power of One, who opened up, as in successive visions, the scenes of renovation. As to the alleged contradiction, so persisted in, between the first and second chapters, it is imaginary. The first chapter is a grand picture of the renovation of the earth for man up to man's creation, introductory not only to the whole Book of Genesis, but to the whole Bible, the preparation of the books of which in the future ages was foreseen by God. The second chapter is a more special account of man as he appeared on the earth in connection with the fall afterwards, picturing him as in fact the lord of creation. It has a distinct aim, and does not contradict the first. The third chapter describes the catastrophe which overtook him, God having created him with a free will, which is essential to a pure intelligence. There is then the brief view of the progress of the early races, culminating in the falling away of the whole race, except the one family, from the worship of God and true morality, till they were destroyed by the flood. Then rapidly we pass on to the history of Abraham, the chosen agent of God for the preservation of light and truth in the world. The rest of the book is occupied with the history of the patriarch and his immediate descendants. There is a clear purpose in the book from its beginning to its close. The object is to introduce the great work of redemption —to be unfolded as the ages passed on—to show the actual position of man as fallen, and the means devised by God from the world's early ages for his restoration. The book was doubtless, we think, *compiled from different documents*, but by Moses, who, from his great knowledge was well-fitted for the task, by his previous training in the learning of Egypt, even as the Apostle Paul was fitted by his early training and preparation to write his Epistles. Its early parts, including the chronologies, must have been known in their substance in the first patriarchal ages; and the histories of the patriarchs Abraham, Isaac, and Jacob may have been written near their own time, much of them very possibly by Joseph, who may also have told his own tale. These records may have existed, being carefully preserved by the Jews in Egypt. Moses during his long residence in Midian, or even earlier in Egypt itself, or later in the wilderness, may have put them together in that form in which we now have them in the Book of Genesis. If we look attentively to the intelligent connection of the book, we find no evidences of incongruity in the uses of the names by which God is described. Elohim is the name of God in connection with His supreme creative power, pointing, certainly, to more than one Person in the Godhead; Jehovah is the name of God in connection with the covenant of grace, exhibiting His special relations to men as covenant God, associated, as we believe, with the Second Person of the Godhead. These names are used in Genesis and elsewhere with perfect *discrimination*, and do not clash, as if one referred to one kind of Deity, and another to another, nor point to opposing documents. They describe God as the Creator and Centre of all power, and God as the covenant God under the work of the redemption. The confusion has arisen in the minds of those who ignore all redemptive work, and do not, and cannot, consequently, understand the spiritual relations implied in the name Jehovah. There is in the Book of Genesis a distinct connection of the parts—the evidence of its preparation, under a higher guidance, by one of clear intellect, who, comparing the different documents, put together the whole narrative. The stories of Abraham, Isaac, and Jacob, and of Joseph, are told with that simplicity which characterizes all the Bible narratives in both the Old Testament and the New, and with none of that bombast and high-flown expression which *always* appear in *myths* and mere human narratives of heroic deeds. This can be seen easily by comparing these simple, plain narratives with the traditions of the Jews about Abraham, Moses, etc., as given in the Talmud.* The Scriptures have *throughout* certain characteristics which it is impossible for the dispassionate mind not to discern. There is quietness; there is strength; there is transparent truthfulness, despite all the assertions of the critics of the naturalistic school, who, of course, can see only confusion in books of which the presence and action of God constitute the main features—which presence and action they are pleased to treat as impossible. The play of *Hamlet* without Hamlet is nothing in comparison. That the other books of the Pentateuch were not only edited, but written, by Moses, as alleged, is not disproved, but is as likely as ever. Those who have lived long in Egypt, and are acquainted minutely with its climate, as well as those who know the desert, attest that no man could have written the Book of Exodus who was a mere visitor or passing traveller, but only one who had lived long in the regions, understood minutely their characteristics, and was perfectly

* See Appendix B.

familiar with them. There are no mistakes in the references of Moses. The greatest Egyptian scholar, Professor Ebers, has written a novel—' An Egyptian Princess '—illustrative of old Egyptian life, remarkably well done, but with many little mistakes, which strikes at once the resident. But there are *no mistakes* of Moses as regards Egypt. Everything manifests long and thorough knowledge of the country. And as to the desert, the route of the Israelites, according to the Mosaic records, can still be clearly traced, as it was by the late Professor Palmer—the greatest colloquial Arabic scholar. There is a large space under Sinai exactly agreeing with the position where the vast congregation was represented to have heard the law. To have supposed some visitor to Egypt and the desert to have written the book, with all the pictorial descriptions of the camp and of events which never happened, is to suppose an absurdity. The narrative is plain and unaffected, describing the most marvellous events without the slightest aiming at effect ; but in calm, life-like language —and in all its references to country, climate, winds, animals, routes, etc., able to stand the most sifting examinations.

The truth is, these naturalistic critics, who start with the idea of accounting for the Old Testament apart from the existence of a living God, have to invent or suppose far greater marvels than they deny. Their credulity, in attempting to force through their own theories, is unbounded.

The following is a quotation from a remarkable article of Dr. Lansing, a well-known American missionary, who has lived many years in Egypt, taken from *The Christian Church*, of which I was editor. After noting a number of mistakes of Ebers, which anyone born and brought up in Egypt would at once detect, he proceeds :

'*No author, or company of authors, who had not spent their lives, or a great portion of their lives, in Egypt, could have written the Pentateuch.*

'In this I do not intend to assert that Moses, in the parts of his history which preceded his own times, did not avail himself of already existing documents; nor yet that during his lifetime others *of his contemporaries* may not have written parts of the Pentateuch, as we have the four Gospels written by the hands of the four Evangelists; nor yet that a few sentences may not have been added by a later and an inspired hand, or crept in from the margin; nor yet that there are not in the Pentateuch certain expressions upon which we are yet needing "more light" (though they are daily becoming less). What I do assert is, that to suppose the Pentateuch (its middle books as well as those at its two ends) was written in Palestine four, six, or eight centuries after the Exodus, and by men who had not resided for long years in Egypt, is as preposterous as it would be to suppose that "Holy Willie's Prayer," or the "Cotter's Saturday Night" were written by a Parisian Frenchman, or "Hiawatha" by an Ashantee chief. The proof of this thesis thus strongly stated might be sought by different authors from standpoints as various as their different modes of thought and lines of study. Some would take the line of good old John Owen, in his "Self-Evidencing Light of the Scriptures"; but I fear they would avail little with the German "higher critics" and the Anglo-Saxon retailers of their crudely assimilated materials. Others would view it from the standpoint of the historical coincidences, such as those so ably set forth in Blunt's work on the "Veracity of the Books of Moses." The standpoint from which I have studied the subject is the double one of *linguistic* and *local*, and with me the general thesis given above resolves itself into two, as follows :

' 1st. The Egyptian words adopted in the Pentateuch, and afterwards incorporated in the Hebrew language, prove the Egyptian origin of the Pentateuch.

' 2nd. The local allusions of the most minute character to Egyptian matters prove that the writer or writers of the Pentateuch had spent the greater portion of their lives in Egypt.'

These two statements, Dr. Lansing established at length in a number of interesting details.

It is to be further noticed that the references to the priesthood and sacrifices, and which are said to be post-exile, are mixed up in the most inextricable way with these accurate descriptions of the desert and of Egypt. The action of the priests and Levites is described in the desert—their functions as to the tabernacle, which Wellhausen says never existed, and their precise conduct in special circumstances —the rebellion and destruction of portions of them, etc. ; all is pictorially before us. The surroundings in the desert, so far as can be tested, are correctly given. The accompanying narratives as to Egypt and the desert can bear closest examination. How then have these been interwoven with post-exile inventions ! The writers must not only have been apt deceivers, thus adroitly binding in the false with the true, but men of wondrous skill, who could do it so perfectly that for many ages the trick remained undiscovered—not even surmised. We are forced to imagine this, if we accept the central idea of the school of criticism by which the priesthood and sacrifices, and separation of priests and

Levites, are brought down to a late date. This can be done only by the supposition, *monstrous from a literary point of view*, that into a narrative which can stand all tests of accuracy as to Egypt, and as to the desert, there have been skilfully interwoven at a late age not only copies of ordinances that did not exist for many ages after, but pictorial descriptions of a tabernacle, and of many actions of priests and Levites, which had not the slightest foundation in fact. Credit it who may, it is an impossible conception from a literary point of view. Fiction has its limits, and such baseless fiction woven beautifully into *narratives that will stand every searching test* is a literary impossibility — an absurd conception which would never have been dreamt of except for the purpose of reconciling the existence of the books with that which is utterly antagonistic to them, viz., abnegation of God and of the supernatural.

It is passing strange that this assertion of the late origin of the priesthood and of the division of priests and Levites has been accepted by many who are believers in God and in inspiration. It is very difficult to understand the position of such, for how could men writing by inspiration of God incorporate inventions which had not the slightest foundation as facts, saying, 'And the Lord spake to Moses,' etc.? Here there is a moral as well as a spiritual impossibility. The truth is that many have been carried away by the mere boldness of the utterances of the naturalistic school. If those who deny God cannot intelligently maintain their position in this matter, as they cannot, much less can those who believe in God and inspiration and the supernatural. *Their* position is *morally* and *spiritually impossible*. The omission at certain periods of references to the priesthood, and the departure from the one-altar law, in certain states of society, can be easily accounted for. The ceremonial law, as well as the Sabbath, was made for man, and not man for the law, and there were many times of convulsion when the nation was so divided and split up by enemies separating its parts that sacrifices would have been impossible on the one-altar system, and the idea of the one altar was always *subordinate* to the essential idea of sacrifice. That Gideon or Jephthah, in a disorganized society, not only surrounded, but actually divided in the heart of the country by enemies, or Elijah after the kingdoms were separated, should have set up altars, and offered sacrifices, even when not priests, is easily accounted for under the circumstances, and does not militate at all against the existence, even from the time of Moses, of a law which was given for a settled state of society. The apparent difficulties arise from a pedantic representation of the ceremonial law as not intended to be accommodated to adverse circumstances, even at times when it could not possibly, in this one matter, be carried out without the abolition of that which was essential, viz., the offering of sacrifices.

The more the subject is considered, the more clearly is it seen that the idea of the late introduction of sacrifices and the priesthood, and of the insertion, not only of the ceremonial laws, but of the alleged facts regarding the existence of the tabernacle and the altars of sacrifice in the wilderness, is one that cannot be maintained. But if this fail, the fabric of this revolutionary criticism falls to pieces. On this theory is based the method of judging the history throughout and the books that record it. For if the priests and the Levites existed in the early times, as described, with the special duties assigned to them, Israel did not develop gradually from a state of barbarism, but were established under the guidance of God by His servant Moses, as a special people, with their own fixed laws and order, from the period alleged in the Pentateuch, when they came out of Egypt and lived in the wilderness—and the wilderness journey and all the events connected with it were literally true. Of course, the higher critics, and all mere naturalists, treat this as impossible, because their standpoint is that there is no revelation or supernatural ; but their attempt to account for the history otherwise than as stated has led them to inextricable confusion, and to suppositions which are perfectly impossible. Even if we put aside moral considerations, the difficulties of introducing into books seen to be ancient and accurate in their references to Egypt and the wilderness, statements not only as to priestly ordinances, but as to priestly actions, made with all the vividness of the ear-witness and eye-witness, are such as cannot be surmounted. The priestly ordinances are given, intermingled with ceremonial and civil laws, and, here and there, with history necessary to explain them, in the last part of Exodus and in Leviticus. In Numbers there is a return to the history, after the Israelites had forsaken Sinai, where God gave them the ordinances, and, later on, an account of their approach to the borders of Canaan. Here again, as in the earlier history, everything is described calmly and with the stamp of truthfulness, and also in perfect harmony with the aspects of the regions through which they passed, and the then condition, so far as known, of the neighbouring nations.

The Book of Deuteronomy, which has been so much assailed, bears the strongest internal evidence of its Mosaic authorship. It is evidently, as seen at a glance, uttered by one recording to a multitude the vivid experiences of many years of scenes witnessed together, in a way which makes the scenes to live before us. It bears the literary marks of this. It is anything but fragmentary. It is continuous and closely connected, passing intelligently from one theme to another, and concluding with fatherly exhortations and warnings as to the future, followed by the magnificent song of praise and by the blessings pronounced on the tribes. It is a thrilling book, with the aspect of dignity, and truth, and holiness inscribed on every part of it—a record and a warning by the father of the people, whose whole spirit is bound to them by the tenderest ties. To say that it was written in Jerusalem many hundred years later by Hilkiah, who had never seen anything that is described, is preposterous. There is the clear impress of the eye-witness—of the leader bound to the people heart and soul by the long memories of the past. There is the dignity of his counsel; there is the earnestness of his purpose; there is the natural and easy reference to the ordinances which the Israelites had received, not going over them minutely, but referring to them as known. There are references also to the marvellous events of the delivery from Egypt and the wilderness journey, and there is fatherly counsel as to the future. If any book ever written bears on it the stamp of historic accuracy, it is this book. As to the laws of the kingdom in Deuteronomy, the objections raised are futile. A kingdom certainly was a possibility when all other nations were governed by kings, and it was wise to give warning as to perils to be avoided in such an event. Besides, by prophetic inspiration, God, through His servant, could give insight into the real events of a future age and prepare for it. As to the last chapter, it was probably written by Joshua—a fitting termination to the Pentateuch of Moses—and let me note that indirectly it implied that the Pentateuch was written by Moses.

The Book of Joshua relates the conquest of Canaan in a strictly historic method. It is full of marvels, but told with no straining at effect, but easily and naturally, as by those who had witnessed them without wonder, because God was recognised as present and giving power. The book proceeds, after the history of the conquest, to give necessary and important minute details as to the division of the country among the tribes in the most matter-of-fact method, and concludes with the death of Joshua. The history proceeds perfectly naturally, in the circumstances, to describe the wars that arose afterwards and the difficulties that beset the people, and though in Judges there is not much said of the priests and Levites, there is plain reference to them, as in the account of Micah the Levite. And then in the Books of Samuel the priesthood and the one sanctuary appear till after the great victory of the Philistines, when the priests were scattered, and Samuel had to offer sacrifices where he could—though principally at Shiloh.

The desire for a king is fully accounted for in the circumstances, as described, of the people, when the enemies of the Israelites within Canaan had become so strong as to be almost masters of the country. There was a want of faith in God in the impatient way in which the people pressed this matter on Samuel, forgetting the many deliverers that had been raised up by God in the past. It was this that was rebuked, and not the mere desire of a king, for God intended the kingdom, and made the kingdom to be a blessing. There is nothing at all difficult to explain in this part of the history, and it requires much less credence to consider it true, unless we deny the existence of God, than to imagine it recorded fictitiously for a purpose in a later age.

In regard to the history of David, there are special evidences of truthfulness in the narratives. David was the great hero of the Jewish nation, associated not only with kingly power, but with inspired song. Whether rightly or wrongly, a large portion of the magnificent Psalms were imputed to him. How can we imagine Jews of a later period, when the halo of David's name had become so great, inventing horrid tales as to David, which were fitted so seriously to injure his reputation? If such an event as that connected with Uriah and Bathsheba had been reported by mere tradition, would not later writers have omitted it or toned it down? What a relief, many people would say now, if we had not this sad catastrophe in David's life! Surely later writers would never have invented such things of the national hero. Is there not literary evidence that a narrative which hides or smooths over nothing that can make the sin repulsive, but describes it in all its moral hideousness—though it was the sin of one praised and celebrated as a great king and true servant of God—was not only a true narrative, recording literally most painful circumstances that occurred, but was also directed by the inspiration of the Spirit, for no *mere human* writer, not overruled by God, would have spoken so plainly? The sins and errors of David are recorded with all plainness, and yet he is called the man after

God's own heart, and praised as one of the most noble and true servants of God that ever lived. Does not this plainness, which is characteristic of the Scriptures throughout, impress upon us absolute truthfulness and Divine guidance?

And here it is fitting to refer to the Psalms. Our faith is not bound up with the authorship of the Psalms. But there is really no ground for upsetting the general Jewish ideas and historic testimony as to the authorship of the Psalms, and the composing of a large portion of them by David, except we accept the theories as to the early history. Of course, if the events recorded in the Pentateuch did not occur, and the ordinances professed to be given there were given for the first time many centuries later, the Psalms must generally have belonged to a later date, for they refer constantly to those events and ordinances, and if, further, God were only known, or evolved, as Kuenen would say, as a living God by the prophets, all the Psalms must belong to a period later than the prophets who evolved the idea of God. 'If,' indeed, but on this 'if' centres the whole position. We have Professor Cheyne, in his recent Bampton Lecture, asserting that almost all the Psalms are of late date, and scarcely one of them a Psalm of David. It is the merest assertion, unless the author adopts the naturalistic theory of Kuenen and others.

There is nothing to show that the Jews were wrong in their traditions as to the authorship of most of the Psalms —traditions, for the most part, seeming to date from the time at which the Psalms were written, and which fit in marvellously with the chequered events as recorded of David's life. Unless we accept the position as to the whole history, there is nothing to interfere with the belief that the

Psalms were written at the periods supposed, and that large portions of them were written by King David. As to one man writing so many Psalms, this is quite in harmony with the history of poetry. One great poet has often written more songs of highest poetic power than had been produced among a whole people for centuries, and the Psalms imputed to David have special characteristics which point to a unity of authorship. They are songs such as the world has never known, revealing the power of spiritual life, but still with the special characteristics of the writers, and most strikingly of one great writer who was full to overflowing of heartfelt devotion to the living and true God—who felt God's mighty loving arm around him in all the varied circumstances of a most chequered life—just such a life as that of David described to us in the history. It is certainly marvellous how many of these Psalms fit into the very periods of David's history with which they are associated in the titles. And David's whole career, more varied than that of any other, eminently fitted him to write hymns adapted to all the most varied circumstances of life.

The different parts of this far-reaching criticism stand or fall together, and it is well to note that the doubts thrown on David's authorship of many of the Psalms are associated with a theory of the history of Israel based on the denial of their knowledge of the one God till the eighth century.

When we consider the prophets, what utter impossibilities, moral and literary, does this criticism create! We surely can judge of the moral tone of writers, to some extent, by their writings. If anything is clear in the character of literature, it is that those who wrote the prophetic books imputed to Isaiah, Jeremiah, Ezekiel, Daniel, and the minor prophets, whoever they were, were men of highest integrity, abhorring lies as the essence of all wickedness, as ruining their own nation in their day; warning against lies of all kinds, declaring God to be a God of absolute truth and righteousness, showing that He contended against and destroyed that which was false and deceptive. There are no such denunciations of lies of every species, and especially of so-called pious frauds, except in the language of Jesus Christ, as in the writings associated with the names of Isaiah, Jeremiah, Ezekiel, Daniel, and other prophets. They speak with indignation and reprobation of the falsehoods practised both politically and religiously, and show that these were the cause of the judgments which threatened or had actually arrived. A religion based on falsehood was, in the words of these prophets, the vilest thing on the face of the earth, as it was afterwards in the words of Jesus. We might quote passage after passage to show this, and we can quote nothing at all to show the contrary—not one single word or expression to defend or extenuate frauds. And yet what is the conclusion to which the so-called higher critics are driven? That these writers, whoever they were, were often acting a false part; that the writings belonged frequently to later dates; that the professed predictions were histories of events that had taken place; that the references to ordinances, which did not exist at the dates given to the books, were put in to bolster up a fraudulent pretence, viz., that these ordinances had come down from earlier times; that the books were full of lies, describing events as of a past age that never occurred; and, further, that those who wrote these books were inventing baseless stories, and palming them off on the people as records and ordinances of Moses, and very often forging the names of former prophets. The writers of these prophecies impress us clearly with the idea that they were men of righteousness and truth—men ready to suffer and die rather than deceive the people. And yet they are to be supposed to be the greatest deceivers, outvying diabolical Jesuitism itself in the manufacture of frauds. The position requires only to be stated to convince one of its worthlessness.

Then as to style. There is apparent in these prophetic writings the individuality of the writers. Fragments are supposed to be put in here and there and everywhere—in Isaiah, for instance. This is necessary to give plausibility to the theories. Some of the critics make ten or twenty Isaiahs. But the writings of Isaiah are most marked for their sublimity of thought, surpassing in this all other writings known. The style is unique and inimitable. This uniqueness and yet identity of style—the same sublime flights of thought and imagination—are to be seen both in the former and latter sections of the prophecy, militating against the idea of even two Isaiahs; but as to the book being a collection of fragments, no one with any literary discernment can maintain it for a moment. In all the prophets, as Jeremiah, Ezekiel, Hosea, Micah, Amos, and others, there is marked unity and individuality. This has been conclusively shown by the Dean of Canterbury, one of our ablest Hebraists.*

But if it is so, they are in many parts distinctly prophetic. To get rid of this we are to suppose that all these prophetic parts were put in after the events had occurred, and then palmed off as ancient. We see to what straits these writers are driven to maintain their theories. They are

* See Appendix C.

unconsciously proving, in their far-fetched explanations, the reality of God and of miracles, which, with efforts so strenuous, in vain they try to get rid of. We have referred to the Book of Daniel, but would note it here again, as it is a central object of attack. Daniel gives most distinct prophecies of the great empires of the world. No one can deny the fitness of his descriptions of the four successive empires, concluding with that of Rome. The words of Daniel descriptive of the Roman Empire, in two distinct prophecies, could not be excelled for accuracy of general delineation. It has long been held by this school of criticism that Daniel must have been written after the period of Antiochus Epiphanes, as he describes so clearly the empire of Alexander the Great, and its divisions on his death, and then the events of Antiochus's reign. But now they are going farther. The description of the Roman power is so clear that the book must have been written after that power was well known—that is, a century or so before Christ. And to this period some late critics impute the book. Now, it happens that Daniel was translated in the Septuagint as a book of the period indicated; but the Septuagint was all completed about two centuries before Christ, and therefore the translators must have used it as a well-authenticated, comparatively ancient book, just after it had issued from the pen of the writer, or, rather, before it had done so. The Jews must have been the most simple and easily deceived people that ever appeared on the face of the earth, in striking contrast to the character they bore, even in the time of their ancestor Jacob, and have borne ever since. The genuineness and authenticity of Daniel have been vindicated by Dr. Pusey in one of the ablest critical books in our language, which has never been answered. There is strongest evidence that it was written by the prophet and statesman Daniel at the periods indicated. The evidences are manifold, and the language is entirely confirmatory, portions being in Chaldee, and portions in Hebrew. Had it been of a late date, it would have been written in Greek, as the books of the Apocrypha. The internal characteristics of the book plainly point to its genuineness and authenticity. It is written in the sublime language of prophecy—written in the highest strain of moral righteousness and truth. It contains also in language of the same prophetic sublimity unmistakable prophecy of the period of the Christ, and of His being condemned to die as a criminal. It is a most genuine book, against which every weapon has been turned, because, unless its testimony can be destroyed, God is *proved* to be the Ruler of all nations at all periods, and consequently, if the book contain true prophecy, the whole fabric of fatalism, and of Agnosticism, and anti-supernaturalism falls to pieces. This book must be destroyed if the destructive criticism is to stand, therefore the strong language used to sweep it away—the assertions again and again made, that its historic position has been overthrown. It has been asserted, and is asserted and re-asserted, that its historic position as the Book of Daniel is now untenable. But the wish is father to the thought. The Book of Daniel stands as firmly at this day as at the moment of the first attack. Its plain prophetic evidence of God being the living Ruler of all nations has not been shaken, and its historic position is immovable. We may note that it is a habit of this naturalistic school to take for granted that positions of especial importance have been destroyed or are about to be destroyed, and thus to alarm people into false concessions, as when an enemy feigns to a garrison that a post has been given up by the main army, in the hope of getting the garrison to surrender. We have constantly to be on the alert against this kind of tactics in dealing with the so-called higher critics.

We have gone thus rapidly through the main positions of attack on the Old Testament. The more we examine, the more clearly do we discern that the theories of the extreme school of critics, by which the Old Testament is turned upside down, are theories which cannot bear examination, which crumble to pieces when put to the test. The shifts to which they are driven in breaking up books, plainly the works of one author, into many fragments, in imputing to men of the loftiest ideas of truth and righteousness, as seen in their writings, the basest and meanest deceptions, in supposing the Jewish nation to have been so simple in matters, in regard to which they were most sensitive, as to be easily imposed on by any frauds; these makeshifts clearly show how difficult, yea, how impossible, it is to account for the books of the Old Testament on any naturalistic basis, and thus indirectly strengthen the position always held in the past, that these books were the productions of the ages to which they professed to belong, were true and honest in their histories, were genuine in their professed prophecies; that they described by a higher influence, breathed upon the writers, the events of future ages, and especially the coming, in the fulness of time, of the great Deliverer.

LECTURE III.

THE HISTORICAL POSITION.—THE DIVINE AND HUMAN IN THE SCRIPTURES: TESTIMONY OF CHRIST TO THEIR FULL INSPIRATION.—MESSIANIC PROPHECIES.—CLOSE CONNECTION OF THE OLD AND NEW TESTAMENTS.—SCIENCE AND MIRACLES.

THE Scriptures of the Old and New Testaments have ever been regarded by the Christian Church as of Divine inspiration, as a revelation made by God to man, and therefore as the infallible rule of faith. All know the position of Judaism, ancient and modern. In ancient Judaism, at the time of our Lord, as shown in the works of Josephus, every portion of the Old Testament Scriptures was regarded as of Divine authority. Enormous pains were taken to secure the accuracy of the copies. The very numbers of words and letters were counted. Our Lord condemned the traditions of the Jews in terms which excited the bitter hatred of the rulers, but the Scriptures He always treated as of *absolute* authority. And the Apostles established from the Old Testament the claims of Christianity. They not only quoted certain passages, but they regarded it throughout as an unerring guide. This authority was also imputed to the New Testament as it appeared. From the earliest period there was no dispute as to inspiration, but only as to the claim of the various books to be considered as Scripture. Not only the Fathers of the Church, but also the heretics, professed to bow before the authority of the Apostolic writings, seeking to prove their positions from them. And so it continued through the Middle Ages. The Jews regarded their Scripture as a Divine revelation, and the Christians, east and west, looked on the Old and New Testaments as throughout a message from God. And thus at the Reformation, when the Reformers assailed as unscriptural many of the dogmas of the Papacy, both sides recognised the authority of the Scriptures. The Roman Catholics also tried to defend their position from it, quoting such passages as 'Thou art Peter, and upon this rock I will build My Church.' The whole Reformation was built up on the idea of the Scripture being *throughout* a revelation from God, and its testimony on every subject indisputable. The theology of the Reformation was constructed on this basis. This position was maintained very generally, though there were a few exceptions, till about fifty years ago. Even the Unitarians of this country did not dispute the authority of the Scripture, but tried, by a new translation, to minimize the effect of passages which seemed to tell against themselves.

Such has been the historical position. The Jewish Church always maintained the inspiration throughout of the Old Testament. Jesus and His Apostles most clearly confirmed this. And the Christian Church accepted from the beginning this position as to the Old Testament, and adopted it as to the New Testament as its books became known, regarding it also as throughout of Divine authority. This continued to be the belief of all branches of the Christian Church till within a comparatively recent period.

It is impossible for man to understand fully the *method* of the Divine inspiration. The living Word, Jesus Christ, was God and Man, but *how?* We do not know, and the written word was of Divine and human origin, but *how* it is not for us to explain. Jesus was truly man—identified with humanity—and yet He was truly God, possessed of Divine power and majesty. 'Great is the mystery of godliness,' 'God was manifest in the flesh '—and it will ever be a mystery. We should need Divine power to comprehend it fully. And so with the Scriptures. They are Divine, and yet they are human, written by men under the influence of the events of the time, with their whole faculties engaged. The characteristics of the different writers are as apparent as those of other authors, and also the circumstances under which they wrote. This was often too much forgotten in the past. The Scriptures were sometimes treated as a mere collection of texts, isolated from each other. Passages were reasoned upon altogether apart from the places in which they occurred, and the connection in which they were found. A great deal of the bitterness of controversy arose from this artificial method of dealing with the Scriptures. Verses were taken out of their connection and pitted against each other. Modern criticism has done a very great service in tracing out clearly the specialities of the writers, and the circumstances connected with the writing of the books. This human element is plainly apparent. The prophets have each their special characteristics—Isaiah was the sublimest poet that ever wrote in any language; David, the most touching lyric-poet that any age has produced. The four Gospels exhibit different orders of minds, each distinct, but St. John, of course, the most marked of all. The personality of St. Paul appears strongly in all his Epistles. The writings, in fact, of the Old and New Testaments bear throughout the distinct marks of their human origin. There is an immense variety in the style of the writers and the order of literature. But though this fact was too often in past ages neglected in searching for the true meaning of passages, it is absurd to suppose that it was not always recognised by men of ability. Luther refers with great clearness and force to the characteristics of different writers, and so does Calvin. All really great commentators make this an important element in guiding them to their interpretations. There is a mistaken tendency in the present day to imagine that so apparent a fact was overlooked, and that we have now entirely new ideas in regard to it. This human element cannot be hidden, and there is no reason for its being hidden. We would say, without any fear of lowering their authority, that the distinctive characteristics of the writers are generally as marked as in any other writings. It is evident that the whole minds of the writers were engaged, that what they wrote proceeded from thought, and knowledge, and inquiry, and feeling. There was a *full*, but not certainly a mechanical, inspiration by which the authors are regarded as mere penmen—a position that is untenable, and that very few have held. The Spirit in directing them used all their faculties and circumstances in accordance with that higher nature to which He had restored them. Nor is this position at all inconsistent nor illogical. The Spirit acts in those whom He quickens, not apart from their faculties, but through them. He brings the intellect, and heart, and emotions into accordance with the will of God, so that while guided by the Spirit they direct their steps with a freedom and elasticity far beyond that of other men, because they have the power as well as the will. If this be the case with the renewed man, why should it not also have been the case, in a more special method, adapted to the work to be done for the Church universal, with the writers of the Divine revelation who were fitted by the Spirit to convey the very message of God?

But, on the other side, the fact of the inspiration or Divine direction is forced upon us even by reason, for while the Scriptures (Old Testament and New) have their human side by which they are specially adapted to influence men— for God speaks to men as men—they have also their Divine aspect, which separates them throughout from all other books ever written. We can easily note proofs of this.

There is a unity, for instance, in their teaching which is perfectly marvellous—truly miraculous—considering the great variety of circumstances under which they were written in so many successive centuries. There is from Genesis to Revelation the same idea of God, as holy, just, and true, and yet merciful, gracious, long-suffering, and kind. There are seldom, even in the New Testament, more touching evidences of the tender love of God than in the history of the patriarchs. This love appears all through the Old Testament. How gracious and long-suffering is God's dealing with the Israelites; how full of the love of God are the Psalms and the prophecies! There is indeed the severity of God against the hardened; but this severity appears with *as much strength* in the language of Jesus, when on earth, as in the Old Testament. Holiness, justice, truth, love, above all are the characteristics of God throughout the whole of these writings, extending, as to their origin, over a period of many centuries.

Then again, as to man, their teaching is the same from first to last. Man is regarded as fallen, as wholly and helplessly sinful, unless he be restored by supernatural influence. For this restoration there needs forgiveness, and therefore sacrifice, which is taught from the beginning, and completed in the sacrifice of Christ on the cross.

Then again, as to Satan and his agents, the books are at one throughout when the subject is referred to—Genesis showing the beginning of the Satanic power among men, and Revelation the close of it.

Thus when we consider the great variety of writers and of circumstances, we have the most evident proof of a guidance in all these writings, which makes them thus harmonious throughout as to the great doctrines they teach.

And again, in all the varied characteristics of the times and the writers, there are certain literary marks in these books which differentiate them from all others. For instance, there is a brevity combined with a wondrous fulness. Some people imagine that there could be no necessity for a Divine guidance in the writing of history—but no idea could be more mistaken. To describe facts truly and tersely is the most remarkable of powers. Now, it is a characteristic of both the Old Testament and the New—that is, *short* passages, they describe the facts of history, not in the method of abstracts, but with most vivid pictorial power. This is strikingly apparent in the Old Testament histories, where men are portrayed as living men with perfect distinctness, often in a few sentences. The greatest historians could not, in many volumes, give such vivid ideas of the the times and the men. We have a clearer view of the character of Ahab and of the kings of Judah and Israel, often in a few sentences, than of Frederick the Great in all Carlyle's volumes, or William III. in all Macaulay's. This could be done only by the guidance of that Spirit who sees into the hearts of all men, and into the deepest currents of all events. The same characteristics appear in historical books of the New Testament. With what brevity, and yet fulness, the four Gospels bring before us sayings and acts of Jesus, avoiding all that is unimportant—not even mentioning once the personal appearance of Jesus—and concentrating attention on that which is important and essential! No men could *possibly have done this except under Divine influence.* The Acts of the Apostles give in the compass of an ordinary tract the most vivid pictures of years of the Church's career in her starting on the great voyage of life. There is thus clear evidence, in both Old Testament and New, of minute Divine guidance even in the historical department, which would seem to need it least of all. No men have ever written, or could of themselves only have written, such histories so brief and yet so full—written with perfect clearness, and with human tenderness and attractiveness—the Spirit acting through the whole souls of the writers, not destroying their individuality, but leading them to express truth with such vividness. What a contrast between their writings and the Jewish traditions, on the one hand, as regards the Old Testament, and the spurious gospels and epistles, on the other, as regards the New Testament!*

But if this higher guidance is plainly seen even in the historic writings, how clear is it in the prophetic, and psalmodic, and epistolary! The prophetic rising often to a great breadth of view and sublimity of conception far above all

---

* See Appendix B.

power of human genius; the psalmodic abounding in appeals most real to the tender love of God and in rhapsodic praise—no mere sentimental expressions, but deep and heartfelt, touching the very springs of life, and exciting devotion intense in all ages since. And then there is the most clear picturing of the future—hundreds or thousands of years before. The attempts made to dispute this are vain and futile. It can be proved with perfect clearness over and over again, both as to the person of the Messiah and the events of His life and death, and as to the events which were to befall different cities and nations. In regard to these predictions it may be said very specially that the prophets desired to look into those things, foretold by themselves. Then as to the Epistles. How different are they from all similar writings, impressing so clearly the great doctrines of the faith with such tenderness and yet such intellectual power! *Everywhere* in Scripture there is the evidence of a superintending power guiding throughout, by inspiring the *whole soul* of each writer, and enabling him not only to state that which was necessary, but also to *abstain* from stating the unnecessary.

There is thus evidence of both the Divine and the human elements, but the Divine not separate from the human, but interpenetrating it, so that every part of the revelation is from God—the idea always recognised in the Jewish and Christian Churches—the writers filled with the Holy Spirit, acting upon all their faculties and bringing forth from them a Divine music suited to their character and circumstances. We hear the voice of St. Peter in his Epistles in distinct harmony with his character and order of mind, and yet there is a higher voice—the voice of God—

using him, with his specialities, as an instrument; and so in the case of all the writers. What more marked than the character of St. John in his Gospels and Epistles, or of St. Paul, in his great grasp of thought, vigorous reasoning, and burning affection? But withal they are under the guidance of a higher Power. Compare the writings of the Fathers, or the Reformers, or any theologians. These take volumes to describe that which is given in sentences.

The position held by the Jewish and Christian Churches —the latter certainly from the beginning, as taught by Jesus and His Apostles—is that the whole Scripture was given by inspiration—a revelation from God—given in a human method by human agents, with all their powers in action and their faculties at work, and therefore with personal characteristics as distinct as those of other writings. It is difficult to understand this. But it is not more difficult than to understand how the perfectly Divine and human acted in harmony in the person of Jesus, and yet this is the centre of our Christian faith. Such problems are beyond our power of explanation—*above*, not *contrary* to reason. If God gives us a revelation at all, it must surely be given as a whole, and not in isolated sections, left to be discovered by ourselves. What God declares must have authority; but the authority is gone if we do not know whether it is from God or not. *Then* supremacy is given not to God, but to our own understanding, which is to find out for itself what is of Divine origin, and what not. How can it find out if not itself supreme? It seems impossible to suppose God giving a revelation in such a method—therefore without authority—leaving men to find out what is agreeable to their own ideas, and what not. Imagine a father giving his child directions in such a method or a State its laws. It would be utterly confusing, and would destroy all authority. And surely the great and infinite God cannot, if He reveal Himself at all, but let us know clearly that the message is His. It will consequently be found that men are very soon driven logically to deny a revelation when they deny the authority *throughout* of the Scriptures. It is a *complete and full* inspiration that we desiderate—and this was the representation and the idea of the Jewish Church beyond all doubt, and of the Christian Church universally till a recent period. But what is of supreme importance is that it received the imprimatur of Jesus in the planting of the Christian Church.

The testimony of Jesus as to the Scriptures is very clear—seen to be the more clear, the more comprehensively we look to His sayings and actions. In the age of our Lord there were three things asserted by the Jewish ecclesiastics : the absolute authority of Scripture ; the authority of tradition ; and the authority of the Church as the interpreter of both. Both of the latter Jesus condemned as false, and thereby roused that bitter antipathy of the rulers which made them to persecute Him to death. They felt that He was a formidable rival—as a worker of the most wondrous miracles, and as a speaker of words which attracted the attention of all. If He succeeded in gaining the ear of the people generally their power would be gone. The conflict was as bitter on their part as that of the Romish Church in the sixteenth century against the Reformers. The very centre of the conflict consisted in Jesus' utter rejection of the authority of tradition and denial of the claims of the Jewish Church to be the infallible, or even a safe, interpreter of Scripture.

And it appears amazing how, except by mere blindness, men professing to be followers of Jesus can maintain the authority of tradition, and the right of the Church, as such, to be the only interpreter of the Scriptures. These were the very points raised at the time of the mission of Christ on earth, and He declared Himself as to them with all clearness. The Jewish Church had a much better claim to be the infallible interpreter of the Old Testament Scriptures than any one of the many sections of Christendom can have to interpret the whole Bible. The claim was condemned by Jesus, cast aside as unholy and unworthy—'Ye make void the law.' The Scriptures were not written for the few, but for the many. They were addressed to the understandings and hearts of men, to be studied indeed with care and diligence, but to be treated intelligibly and clearly, not as mystic signs or hieroglyphs. Our Lord opened *the understanding* of the Apostles on the day of His resurrection, and showed clearly and intelligently the references to His own mission. And the Apostles did the same in spreading abroad Christianity. They showed not blindly nor superstitiously, but clearly and vigorously, by intelligent reasoning, how the Old Testament led up to Jesus—the promised Messiah. Interpretations as of *mere blind authority* were *never* put forward. We see this in a perusal of the Epistles. Such despotic ecclesiasticism Jesus had condemned in the strongest terms, and certainly did not purpose to establish in His Church. He also spoke with withering scorn of the authority of traditions, even the most ancient. He would not wash His hands before meat, because by a tradition it had been made a superstitious observance. Popular superstition He strenuously opposed.

Yet in the face of this action of our Lord, both as regards

a blind ecclesiasticism and the authority of tradition—action which led the rulers resolutely to plot His death—we have the astonishing assertion that Jesus' language about Scripture was *in accordance with popular prejudice*—that He *accommodated His teaching to the weaknesses of the people.* Nothing could be more contrary to the facts—as well as derogatory to His character and work : He did not do so, but went in direct opposition to the teaching of His age. He opposed and condemned, plainly and clearly, traditionalism and a false ecclesiasticism. Therefore there is *no ground whatever* for the statement that, in speaking of the Scriptures as He did, He *accommodated Himself to the mistaken ideas and prejudices* of the age. Had Jesus considered the Jewish idea of the Scriptures, as possessed *throughout* of Divine authority, to be false, He would, undoubtedly, in harmony with His other action as to tradition and ecclesiasticism, have shown to the people their error, have condemned what has been termed in modern times bibliolatry. But He never did so. He confirmed the people in their reverence for Scripture. He treated it always as of *absolute* authority. He spoke so strongly as to say that if they believed not Moses and the prophets, neither would they believe though one rose from the dead. He showed in the inner circle of His disciples how the various facts of His life were foretold in the Scriptures. He said that not one jot or tittle should fail. He set up the Scriptures against tradition and against ecclesiasticism. And no sooner had He risen from the dead than, without a day's delay, He expounded to them *intelligently* the Scriptures, opening their *understanding*, and sending them forth to convert the world with the testimony of Scripture in their hands. As instructed by Jesus, the

Apostles, from the beginning, even in the Gentile Church, introduced the reading of the Old Testament Scriptures as the authoritative word of God. Thus, on the one hand, Jesus did not ever speak in the language of the mistaken ideas of His age, for He denounced in unmeasured terms the great popular delusions of the day of the Jewish Church; and, on the other, He clearly accepted the authority of the writings of the Old Testament in *all their parts*, so that *simply to quote* from them was sufficient to establish a position as Divinely true; and He sent forth His messengers to found on them His claims to be recognised as the Saviour of men, both of Jews and of Gentiles. The vague statements of many writers on the subject need only to be sifted to show their groundlessness.*

Many have attempted further to say that Jesus may Himself have been mistaken. No idea can be more repulsive or subversive of faith. If Jesus—filled with the Holy Ghost —as the messenger of God, Himself the Son of God, was mistaken, where is there any security for any part of Christianity? 'If I have told you earthly things, and ye believe not, how shall ye believe, if I tell you heavenly things?' If He were mistaken as to the great question of the authority of the Scriptures, how can we rely on His statements as to the future—'the many mansions' which He has gone to prepare for His redeemed? Such statements are contrary to all ideas of Jesus as the Son of God, and the ideas of every age and place where that doctrine has been accepted,

* The question as to the recognition of the Scriptures by our Lord is concerned not with mere details, but with His whole method of treating them. He regarded them, without doubt, as of Divine authority throughout, so that to quote the Scriptures intelligently was sufficient to establish any position. Could He have so treated them if many parts of them had been lies and inventions?

and cannot but lead logically to Socinianism, or worse. The idea that Jesus did not know exactly the position in relation to God of the Old Testament and its writers is destructive of His claims as the Divine Messenger of heaven, who Himself spake through the prophets, and gave forth through the Spirit the word of God to men.

There can be no doubt that the Jews, in consequence of the prophecies, were expecting a Messiah about the time that Jesus appeared. This is not only stated in the New Testament, but in Josephus, and in the traditions which were reduced to writing at a later period in the Talmud. The Jews never doubted that the *ancient prophets* were enabled by God to foretell many events of the future as regarded both themselves and other nations. The whole country of Judæa and of Galilee was in eager expectation of the promised Deliverer. When the rumour came of the wise men from the East, and Herod gathered together the scribes and men of learning of the Jews, they had no doubt of the coming of the Messiah, and knew accurately the place where He was to be born. We can trace with perfect ease the grounds of this belief. The Old Testament was, fortunately, translated into Greek hundreds of years before the time of our Lord, so that there can be no question of the genuineness of the text where it is supported both by the Hebrew and the Greek versions, as these were independent documents in the hands of the Jews—the bitter enemies of Christ and Christianity. Many of these books speak so plainly on this subject of the Messiah that, if there had been a possibility, these modern critics would, unquestionably, have imputed passages to Christian interpolations. There is no possibility of this, so they attempt to explain them away altogether. But there they are—most plainly written—interspersed through many books of the

Old Testament. There was Moses' prophecy of that 'prophet,' which was universally believed by the Jews to point to the Messiah. There were the promises to David, and the numerous references to the family of David, even long after that family had ceased to reign. These references to a wondrous Successor of that family appear in later prophecies as well as in earlier. There was the clear statement that One of great power and majesty should arise as the Prince of the people—one descended from David. The place of His birth was pointed out. The time was approximately given, especially in the Book of Daniel. The sufferings of the Christ were described in different parts, in passages considered by the Jews themselves as Messianic, though, after the spread of Christianity, they attempted to explain them otherwise. Most of the portions of the Old Testament regarded as Messianic in the Christian Church were so regarded by the Jews before, and during, the age in which Christ lived. Thus the Old Testament was, and is, intimately bound up with the New. It is a book which, in innumerable places, refers to the Christ. That this is no imagination is proved by the undoubted fact that the Jewish nation, founding on such prophecies, universally expected a Messiah. Whence this expectation? It came from the predictions of the Old Testament. This they avowed, and they were ready to state the reasons for their expectation.

While Jesus rejected traditions and ecclesiastical pretences, He accepted most fully the idea of numerous prophecies applying to Himself. After the resurrection, He expounded, on the evening of the day, with great fulness, the things written in the prophecies concerning Himself. To the two whom He met on the way to Emmaus He said:

'O foolish and slow of heart to believe all that the prophets have spoken! Behoved it not the Christ to suffer these things, and to enter into glory. And, beginning from Moses and all the prophets, He interpreted to them in all the Scriptures the things concerning Himself.' And on the same evening as the eleven and others were gathered together, He said unto them : 'These are My words which I spake unto you while I was yet with you, how that all things must needs be fulfilled which are written in the law of Moses and the prophets and the Psalms concerning Me. Then opened He their understanding, that they might understand the Scriptures ; and He said unto them, Thus it is written, that the Christ should suffer, and rise again from the dead the third day, and that repentance and remission of sins should be preached in His name unto all the nations, beginning at Jerusalem.'

And as Jesus directed them, His Apostles sought to establish everywhere His claim to the Messiahship from the Old Testament. Christianity was not a superstition. It was, and is, a *reasonable*, intelligent religion, resting on evidence—and no evidence more important than the clear announcements and preparations for it in the Old Testament. This was the method of attesting its claims to the Jews always, and of seeking to win them over intelligently to it. St. Peter, on the Day of Pentecost, quoted the prophecy of Joel as indicating the events that had taken place on that day ; and then, referring to Jesus as well known to them by mighty works and wondrous signs, spoke of His resurrection, and quoted the reference to it in the 16th Psalm, showing clearly that the words of that psalm could not refer to David himself. When St. Paul entered on his great mission, though his mission was specially to the Gentiles, he went always first to the Jews, and he brought many of them over to Christianity. How? By showing intelligently from the prophecies of the Old Testament that Jesus was the Christ, foretold ages before. And so with all the Apostles and preachers this was the method adopted throughout to convince the Jews. And even in the Gentile Church the reading of the Old Testament was at once introduced as a part of the service. It was read, we know, regularly in the early Christian gatherings, not only of Jews, but of Gentiles; and it was esteemed by the whole Christian Church as of absolute authority. The Psalms and prophecies especially were much dwelt upon as indicating to the Gentiles, as well as to the Jews, that God had prepared the world for the coming of Jesus by announcing His advent, and sufferings, and death and resurrection, and ascension, through His prophets—ages before He appeared. Those who would undermine the Old Testament as a trustworthy, not to speak of inspired, record, would remove that by which the claims of Christ and Christianity were established at first. They would destroy the *sources from which Jesus Himself and the Apostles and the Church in its first age* derived the evidence of His mission.

The word of God is bound together from the beginning, to the end, and it is a revelation of Christ. The Scripture, though composed of many books of many periods, is one whole. At the very beginning it describes the position of man as having become abnormal by sin, and points to the need of sacrifice and redemption. The whole system of sacrifice had a meaning even before the special ceremonial laws were given to the Jews. This appears in the sacrifice of Abel. It appears in various sacrifices in Genesis. But it appears also in many of the sacrificial systems of other nations, plainly indicating the early origin, not only of sacrifice, but of its significant lessons. The whole system of sacrifice had a meaning from the beginning; but the detailed ceremonial laws of the Jews were full of meaning, which spiritual Jews saw—*as indicated* and stated indeed, in many of the Psalms and prophecies. The Old Testament system is in harmony with that of the New Testament, which was its completion or fulfilment. This is shown with great clearness in the Epistle to the Hebrews, which begins by proving from varied passages of the Old Testament the foretelling of the Divine, and also the human, nature of Christ, and then goes on to show how the sacrificial system symbolized the work He was to accomplish for forgiveness of sin, and also His heavenly priesthood. We may say that the ceremonial law of the Jews was one great prophecy throughout, as shown in the well-known book of Dr. Andrew Bonar on Leviticus—in 'Notes on Exodus,' and 'Leviticus,' and other works. The ordinances of the Jews were a preparation for the coming of Christ, and were fulfilled in Him, in His sacrifice and death, and in His heavenly glory. Thus Christianity itself is closely bound up with the truth of the Old Testament, which many speak of as of little importance to it. The assault is not only against the Old Testament, but against the great Divine and supernatural system with which it is associated, and which culminated in the appearance and acts and victories of Jesus of Nazareth. If the authority of the Old Testament could be destroyed, Christianity would be shaken to its foundations.

Holy men of God spake as they were moved by the Holy Ghost. This is now inverted by the critics, who declare that unholy men devised, under a pretentious sanctity, all kinds of forgeries by which to deceive the people; that they interpolated designedly false statements here and there to throw them off the scent; and that they palmed off on the people historic narratives as old predictions—a most base offence. Kuenen says: 'The Israelitish priesthood, to maintain its authority and heighten its prestige, employed the same means which priests used elsewhere in the old world, and of which the Bishops of Rome made use in the middle ages in the forged decretals. This fact must be acknowledged in its full scope and significance. But while we do this, we wish, at the same time, to bear in mind that such "pious frauds" were considered lawful. It appears therefore that the Jews, upon the whole, had other notions of literary good faith than we have. They saw nothing reprehensible in the use of borrowed means; the only question was whether they used them to a good purpose.' This statement of Kuenen is an utterly baseless assumption, of which the documents or history give not the slightest indications.

We can understand such a position taken up by naturalists, who, in their desperation to establish an untenable position, cannot otherwise get rid of the supernatural, but how anyone can profess to say that the Old Testament is inspired and is full of all kinds of deception passes comprehension. There must surely be some secret meaning in their use of the word 'inspiration.' A story is told of Kuenen, which, if not true, as we believe it is, is well invented. He is said to have expressed himself as to a certain well-known critic in this country: 'It is quite true that I impute forgeries, but I never charge them on the Almighty.' The position of those who accept these tricks and forgeries, and yet say they believe the writers to have been inspired, passes comprehension. Surely they ought to explain themselves more clearly.

There are, all through the Old Testament, sublime prophecies of the coming of the Messiah and the glory of His kingdom. Isaiah celebrates in unmistakable language the going forth through the Messiah of the word of the Lord to the ends of the earth. This is seen in many parts of the prophecy from the beginning onwards, as beautifully in the thirty-fifth chapter: 'The wilderness and the solitary place shall be glad for them, and the desert shall rejoice and blossom as the rose. It shall blossom abundantly, and rejoice even with joy and singing; the glory of Lebanon shall be given to it, and the excellency of Carmel and Sharon.' And how pointedly in the eleventh chapter!—'And it shall come to pass in that day that the *Root* of Jesse shall stand for an ensign of the peoples; unto Him shall the gathering of the nations be.' How sublimely in the second chapter!— 'And it shall come to pass in the last days that the mountain of the Lord's house shall be established in the top of the mountains, and shall be exalted above the hills, and all nations shall flow unto it. And many peoples shall go and say, Come ye, and let us go up to the mountain of the Lord, to the house of the God of Jacob, and He will teach us His ways, and we will walk in His paths. And He shall judge between the nations, and shall reprove many peoples; and they shall beat their swords into plowshares and their spears into pruning-hooks: nation shall not lift up sword against nation, neither shall they learn war any more.' There are all through this prophet's writings references to the glorious future of the world under the Messiah. But from the fortieth chapter to the sixty-sixth, which is a prophecy of the Messiah from beginning to end, written at a later period of life, but we believe by the same person, because there is a sublimity of style in both exactly similar, but differing from the style of the other prophets—in this second portion what a view is given of the mission and the majesty of the Deliverer: 'Comfort ye, comfort ye, My people, saith your God.' Then the voice of preparation in the wilderness; then the certainty of the fulfilment of God's promises, not temporary, as the grass and the flower, but eternal; then the Divine majesty of the Promised One: 'Behold, the Lord God shall come as a mighty One, and His arm shall rule for Him; behold His reward is with Him, and His recompense before Him. He shall feed His flock like a shepherd; He shall gather the lambs in His arms, and carry them in His bosom, and shall gently lead them that give suck.' Then His almighty power as Creator of all things—told in the sublimest words ever penned; then the appeal to the fulfilment in the past of God's prophetic utterances; and then the description of Jesus in His human aspect as He appeared among men: 'Behold My servant whom I uphold, My chosen in whom My soul delighteth; I have put My spirit upon Him; He shall bring forth judgment to the Gentiles.' Then the commission: 'I the Lord have called Thee in righteousness, and will hold Thine hand, and will keep Thee, and give Thee for a covenant of the people, for a light of the Gentiles; to open the blind eyes, to bring out the prisoners from the dungeon, and them that sit in darkness out of the prison-house.' And so this sublime prophecy goes on, sweeping before it the affairs of the nations, showing the preparation, remote and near, for the advent of the King, bringing Him forth in all His might, but also in His passage through the dark valley—'Who hath believed our report?'—as He approaches His humiliation and death. Can it be that the Mighty One is thus to suffer? Yes, because He bare the sins of many. Through His sufferings are men to be delivered. And so the prophecy flows on to the end, describing the messenger and the message, and its effects, until the whole earth shall be filled with His glory—the Jews shall be restored, and all nations shall worship Him.

Not only is Christ and Christianity prophesied of in the Old Testament in whole sections of prophecy as well as in individual passages, but many parts of His conflict and mission are more fully described there than in the New Testament, which was designed by the Spirit of God to be a completion of the Old Testament, and does not therefore repeat all those things which the Old Testament supplies. Thus many Psalms describe the conflicts and express the feelings of the soul of Christ in the pilgrimage of life, in every variety of circumstance. There are in the prophetic Psalms—as the 2nd, the 22nd, the 45th, the 72nd, the 110th, and many others—descriptions of the work, and mission, and power of Christ of the most vivid kind. In the 22nd Psalm we read not only accurately of the events that took place at the cross, but we have a description of the soul-sufferings of Christ, when He became sin for us, such as we have not in any part of the New Testament. In the 72nd Psalm there is the most searching picture of the character of His kingdom, of its liberty and its peace, of its happiness and prosperity. Thus the Old Testament does not only prophesy of Him, but it throws great light on His contests, His distresses, His joys, and His victories. In the words of the Old Testament we find often the language best adapted to describe the person of Jesus and the blessedness of His mission. Much of that which fills up the outlines, and gives to the facts life and reality, we find in the Old Testament. There is thus clear internal evidence of the same Spirit speaking in both. And this is the true representation—Christ the Centre of all Scriptural teaching.

Jesus' mission to the earth was not a passing event. He was and is the Light of the world—the Light of all the ages of the world—of all the nations. His appearance was not an isolated fact. It was that round which the history of the world from beginning to end revolves. The Old Testament, not only in isolated prophecies, nor in symbols, but in men raised up as representatives of Him, in its teaching and connection, prepared for and foretold Him. It was the Spirit of Christ Himself that spoke by the prophets. And we have no complete picture of Him, unless we associate the Old Testament with the New.

Those who view the life of Jesus on earth apart from the light thrown on it by the prophetic spirit of the Old Testament have a most imperfect view. The life of Jesus itself, with His words and deeds as given in the Gospels, is the most interesting of all themes; but when looked at as isolated we cannot understand it. Thus those 'Lives of Christ' written by unbelievers are so unreal and barren. He lived a truly human life on earth, and every incident of it is of deepest interest. We never can read it but we see something new; but there is immense additional light thrown on it by the Psalms and prophecies, which bring out easily and naturally its import and its relation to the history of all ages, and which cast around it the halo of the heavenly glory. Through Jesus' true manhood we see His Godhead; but when we view His life as that of only a man, we cannot possibly feel its power or perfection. The claims that He made of absolute knowledge, of equality with God, of being the Light of the world, so far from indicating perfection, would indicate mad presumption in anyone who was only one of the countless millions of the human family that have been born and died on earth. The perfection of His nature can be seen only when we associate it with His true Godhead. Then His vast unbounded claims to knowledge, position and authority, to be the Sun of the human system, are natural and necessary.

His life was the central event in human history, that around which all other events revolve. Before He came men were waiting for His advent, and the Jewish nation was through the prophets kept in bright expectancy of the future—yea, even the patriarchs were so: 'Your father Abraham rejoiced to see My day, and he saw it and was glad.' And after He appeared, His power, that of the humble Galilean of Nazareth, as He was supposed to be, living in poverty and lowliness, continued to spread abroad through all countries. His kingdom shall yet fill the whole earth, as clearly foretold. His kingdom is an everlasting kingdom, and His dominion that which shall never come to an end.

The Old Testament and the New are bound together as a *living organism*, and the lowering of the authority of the Old Testament must necessarily lead to the undermining of Christianity. The same kinds of attack have been made against both, and from the same sources. The attempt is made still by many to account for the New Testament apart from the supernatural. Those men who have embraced naturalism in any form—Agnosticism, Materialism, or any other, cannot permit the idea of the supernatural. It is excluded, without saying. Everthing must be toned down and explained away so as to admit of a natural, matter-of-fact, every-day explanation. Neither Jesus nor the Apostles ever saw or did a miracle. All that has been written about miracles is unfounded. The resurrection itself, on which the existence of Christianity turns, never took place. This view of the New Testament is still as widespread as the naturalism on which it is founded. It is no doubt at all the view of Kuenen and Wellhausen, and those who are, with the same weapons, undermining the Old Testament. Baurism has failed in its details, though the ablest of all attempts to account for the New Testament on natural principles; but that which gave rise to Baur's effort is as rampant as ever, and the same men who deny the supernatural in the Old Testament deny the supernatural in the New, and treat with scorn the idea of the resurrection and ascension of our Lord.

There are some good earnest men in this country of even the revivalist school who do not at all understand the question, and who are inclined to let the destructive criticism have its way with many parts of the Old Testament if only you leave them the New—in fact, they say they are thus driven more to depend on the person and work of

Christ. This is an utter delusion, arising from ignorance of the nature of the controversy. The same weapons turned against the Old Testament, and by the use of which alone its position appears to be shaken, with equal power assail the miracles of Jesus and His resurrection and ascension. Those who are at the head of this school of criticism do not believe in the incarnation or the resurrection of Christ, or in Christianity as anything but a natural outcome of human thought and progress. If the basis of the criticism—that which alone gives it any weight—is correct, Christianity logically disappears as a revealed religion.

The battle is thus not against the Old Testament only. This is but one phase of it. It is against all supernatural religion. It regards everything as unknowable except what we observe by our own faculties, and would make a clean sweep of all that is above the powers and reason of man. It treats all history alike, and no matter what the evidence for miracles, it regards it as worthless. It takes for granted that all miracles are fabulous. It thus attempts to obliterate the leading features of the Old and New Testaments, and to leave Christianity no foundation.

Let us now examine the basis of this criticism. Are miracles to be set aside? Has it been proved that the order of the world goes on through mere natural laws, working themselves out by an internal development, and with no possibility of interference by a Higher Power, and, indeed, no higher Power, conscious and intelligent, to control them? Much folly has been given utterance to on this subject. We are told that science has decided it. *Science has not even touched it.* The object of science is to trace out the physical laws that control phenomena. Science has made vast progress in recent times, and seems to be but at the beginning of discovery. No one can undervalue the great services of science or fail to be struck with its wondrous results. But science does not interfere with religion, nor take the place of religion, nor *assert anything* at all in *regard* to the *great spiritual world*. The Bible has not those contradictions to the discoveries of science which appear flagrantly in all heathen representations of the world and creation. There is, even in this, evidence of the controlling Divine power, called inspiration, in the minds of the writers. No sublimer or grander idea could be given of the heavens, with all our modern discoveries, than in the language of certain Psalms and of the prophet Isaiah. There is not a hint of those theories, probably prevalent at the time among the Jews as others, which make the highest cosmogony—that of the cultivated Greeks—ridiculous in the light of modern knowledge. But science has its limits, within which its authority, when the facts are proved, is absolute. It is concerned with the material universe, and the active forces, or laws, which control it. This is its chief function. It may also consider the phenomena of mind. But its knowledge of these is acquired only from observation and induction. It does not go into the heart of things or explain anything beyond. Some scientists of extreme views say that there is no knowledge but that acquired from observation, and that therefore science comprehends all knowledge; but this is to take for granted what is plainly unfounded. The great majority of scientific men believe in a spiritual world, and many of the ablest scientists are firm believers in the revelation of God in His word, and see nothing whatever in such belief inconsistent with their knowledge of science. We grant what is untenable if we consider that science opposes revelation. It is not so. It opposes superstition. It unfolds the order of the universe. It makes us to see that the same laws that act in our world act in distant space. But it does not deny in any respect an intelligent Creator. Nay! as has been so ably shown by the Duke of Argyll, in his ' Unity of Nature,' it establishes more strongly than ever the idea of a Divine controlling intelligence. The order of nature is not a material, lifeless order; it is the most intelligent adaptation of means to ends by thought and contrivance similar in kind to that, but infinitely greater, which is possessed by the human soul. The sphere of inquiry has been enormously enlarged since the time of Paley; but more clearly and wonderfully than ever has it been seen that the material universe has been planned and arranged by One who accurately adapts means to ends. Even orders of beings, of the animal and vegetable kingdoms, quite distinct—as insects and flowers—are found, to be adapted to each other's purposes, with the most wonderfully accurate contrivance. The question is, whether there is an intelligent Creator and Ruler of the universe or not. The evidence is *strong as ever* for the existence of such a Being, and there is not one particle of evidence against it. But if there be a living intelligent Ruler of the universe, why may He not make Himself known, and control the works He has made? Even men control material things, and shall God not do so? The Agnostic position has no really intelligent basis, for if God, even possibly, may exist as the Ruler of the universe, how can a creature of limited power assert that He cannot make Himself known by a revelation? It is surely the merest presumption to make such assertion. Man acts upon and moulds the material world to His purposes, and shall not God do so? His slightest interference by whatever means may be a miracle to us. To the barbarian the power that we have acquired by electricity, etc., appears miraculous, and may not God, the Ruler of all, if He exist—and the Agnostics do not deny that He *may* exist—make Himself known by wonderful acts that may be done possibly by controlling one law through another? The position, therefore, that miracles are impossible, unless men are atheists and can from their little centres clearly and intelligently prove there is no God, is mere assertion. It is not intelligent, but unintelligent and irrational. It is the part of a weak, and not of a wise man, to make strong statements about things beyond the range of intellect.

The presumption that all miracles are to be set aside without inquiry is an unintelligent *assumption*, having no basis in reason or in science, or anywhere. It is dogmatism—as much dogmatism as when the Pope asserts his infallibility. Science has made no statement on the subject. It has unfolded, in the most wonderful manner, the universal adaptation intelligently of means to ends all through creation, and has thus impressed, more and more, the idea of a universal Ruler of all things; but it has given no verdict as to miracles. The science of history, which is connected with intelligent acts of men, has *proved*, we think, that there is a *just* Ruler of the world, who punishes the acts of the wicked, as well as rewards those of the righteous. Conscience also asserts the existence of a just Ruler. But science, so far as regards the material universe,

THE ARGUMENT FROM EVOLUTION. 73

says nothing, except to bring to light the intelligent adaptation all through nature of means to ends.

To assert, then, that science has exploded miracles and prophecy, and to pretend that with its light in their hand men may, without argument, cast aside all professed miracles as false, is sheer dogmatism. Theories of the universe have been put forward to support this position, but these theories have nothing to do with genuine science. Evolution, as a broad, all-embracing philosophy accounting for the universe, has not been even made likely in any one department of knowledge. Even if it were established in large circles of knowledge, how, without intelligence, were those laws fixed at first which have directed and regulated the evolution ever since? It only removes the difficulty as to causes further back. But evolution, as a *philosophy of the universe*, has almost no support at all in science. It is exploded in many departments where it made large assertions. It has less apparent likelihood now than ever, and is generally given up, we believe, by scientific specialists. But even if it were proved as a universal principle of action, it would not render miracles impossible. If God created the laws at first, *where* is *He* now, and why should He not act in these ages as He did in a remote past? and if God acts directly, revelation and miracles and prophecy are all possible. Evolution itself takes for granted, if there be a God, that He understands and knows the most distant future, and if He knows, why should He not declare it by the mouths of prophets, when it suits His purposes to do so?

On any theory except that of blank atheism, and it must be an intelligently proved atheism, the ignoring of miracles and prophecy—the treating of them as false *ipso facto*—is mere assumption. But these critics proceed avowedly to deal with the Old Testament on this enormous assumption, as if it had been proved, and were unquestionable. They treat the histories of great miracles, told with apparent truthfulness, and the prophecies of the future, uttered in words of utmost sublimity and moral grandeur, as if they were imaginations or frauds. Bowing down to this baseless theory as a god, they ignore all the historic testimony and all the internal evidence from the spirit and character of the writers.

LECTURE IV.

EFFECT OF THIS REVOLUTIONARY CRITICISM ON THE CHURCHES.

THE effect of this criticism, based on the denial of the supernatural, if believed in, must be destructive of Christianity. If students are taught in our halls of theology that the Old Testament is unreliable ; that large portions of it are made up of fictions palmed off as truth ; that the professed prophecies are statements of events that had taken place—basely put into the form of prophecy, and imputed by deceit (for there is no other way of explaining it) to a past age ; that the prophecies of the Messiah, recognised as such before they were accomplished, and always since by the Christian Church, as those of Isaiah—even the wondrous fifty-third chapter—are only fancifully applied to Christ, and have no bearing on His life and mission—if such positions be taught and maintained, with what message can the preachers go forth to the people ? They may have culture and literary taste, but of what are they to speak ? The same methods can be applied, and have been applied, to the New Testament. The professed account of miracles—of miracles attested not only in the Gospels, but in the earliest Epistles of St. Paul, as facts of constant occurrence—is, forsooth, a delusion and a deception.

The New Testament is not to be trusted. It contains also accounts of prophecies in the Epistles, the Gospels, and the Apocalypse, which last is a professed prophecy throughout. St. Paul refers clearly to the gifts of prophets, of which he had been a witness. The New Testament is therefore, tested by this so-called 'higher criticism,' just as mistaken as the Old. And as to the central fact of the resurrection—the most stupendous of all the miracles except the Incarnation, on which the truth of Christianity absolutely depends, and which the destructive Old Testament critics of Germany laugh to scorn as much as Huxley does—it is as easily swept away as the rest by the method applied ruthlessly to the Old Testament, and it depends much upon cumulative evidence arising from the whole position given to Jesus as the foretold Messiah and the Son of God. Throw doubts on the Old Testament—cast aside its prophecies—treat its alleged historic facts as inventions—assert or imply that the references of the Apostles to it as bearing witness of Him are delusive—inculcate that the writers of it were guilty of every kind of literary fraud, palming off on the nation, as descending from a remote age, a whole system of priestly ordinances which they had introduced themselves—if these things be true, where is there any certainty in any part of Scripture? Let preachers be sent forth from our schools of theology with these doubts in their minds, and what must be the consequence? What have they to declare, and how can they give forth a certain sound on anything? The whole *power* of preaching depends on the *reality* of that which is preached. It is therefore that men will listen with intense earnestness to the sincere statement of things of which they have heard often before, but which fill them with new joy each time that they hear of them again, and for the maintenance of which they would willingly die, because they are connected by a real love to Christ and the hope of a glorious immortality. When preachers speak with certainty on these things, their words will be listened to with interest. But if taught and convinced that the Old Testament, to which Jesus appealed, and the New, are all uncertain, what have men to preach but dreamy speculations? In these days, when literary culture is so widespread, and the daily newspaper is in the hands of all, as well as monthly magazines and reviews, it requires no prophet's power to foretell that, as has happened in other countries, our churches will speedily be forsaken, if our preachers have no certainty as to the reality of the facts and truths attested in Scripture. People will come together not to be stirred up to devotion to Christ, but to listen, as critics, to something that may gratify taste or may not. There is nothing so dead as the worship of our Reformed Churches where it is not instinct with spiritual life and reality—nothing so living where it is. But how can it be instinct with life and reality when the preachers are in doubt as to the truth, or otherwise, of the documents from which they derive their message? It is, therefore, quite certain that if these ideas of the Old Testament, founded on a criticism which has for its basis an infidel philosophy, become general among ministers of the Churches, those Churches will rapidly decay, and Christianity itself will be looked upon as a mere human device. This is no mere imagination, for it is startling to find the number of people, in all the Churches, who, through doubting the truth and reality of the Scriptures, have lost faith in Christianity as a revelation of God, and in Christ as the Son of God, who became man, who suffered and died, the just for the unjust, and who rose from the dead and ascended on high. There is prevalent, through the spread of such false and mistaken ideas of the Bible, a latent Socinianism, and often atheism, which classes Jesus with Buddha or Mohammed, and considers Christianity as a mere human religion, having no truth or certainty as to the future and eternal world. This mistrust of the Scriptures becomes in a Church like a dry-rot in a building—gradually eating away all the material till there is nothing left but crumbling dust. It is therefore of essential importance, if our British and American Protestant Churches are to retain that life and activity which has given them such vast influence for good in the world, that this destructive criticism should be searched into, and its sources made apparent. It is a matter of life and death to the Christian faith, that our well-founded belief in the Scriptures as the word of God be retained. Thus only can preachers speak with certainty, and it is only when they can speak with certainty of living realities, of which they have no doubt, that they can touch the hearts and consciences of others. If the trumpet give an uncertain sound, who will prepare himself for the battle? If the preachers speak of mere speculations, whose heart will be moved and whose soul will be touched? Christianity is all-powerful, because it speaks of facts and of truths which are as real as any events in daily life. If it does not do so, it is dead.

The state of Protestantism in many parts of Germany clearly gives warning of that to which this method of dealing with the Scriptures must lead. In large portions of Protestant Germany the Bible has become an almost unread book, and the churches are deserted. In a Protestant town of 7,000 or 8,000 people, where I attended the university for for a time, the only Protestant Church, which might have held about 2,000, was attended by 100 to 200 at the one service in the week—on Sunday morning. On Easter Sunday it might be filled, but on other Sundays it was almost empty, and there was no other church to attend. It is well known that the proportion attending places of worship in Berlin, and most of the other cities and towns of Germany, is infinitesimal in relation to the Protestant population, scarcely above one or two per cent., while the theatres and halls of amusement and entertainment on the Sundays fill to overflowing. It is so, also, in most parts of Protestant Switzerland. Many of the preachers don't believe in the authority of the Scriptures. They treat the miracles and many portions of the sacred narratives as fables—they preach a formal morality. The people vote for them at election of pastors, but they do not go to hear them. There is no interest in such lifeless addresses. The whole mass of the people become sunk in materialism, fighting the battle of life without religion, and going down to the grave in darkness. God has saved our Anglo-Saxon countries from such calamity, because He has raised up among us, one after another, faithful and earnest men who have touched the very souls of the people, and become the means of bringing many to a sense of the reality of heavenly things; but such preachers have been, without exception, those who have believed with all their hearts in the Bible as the message of God throughout, and who have used it in its various parts as God's designed means for the saving of men. The whole vitality and power of our religion, which has sent forth its great missions to the ends of the earth, has arisen from its Scriptural basis—its belief in the reality of those truths brought to light, not only in the New Testament, but foreshadowed and, more or less, clearly *seen in the Old.*

There is a very great danger of rapid decline at the present time, in connection with these revolutionary views of Scripture. The faith of many is being sorely tried. Churches which had been much blessed and prospered, even in recent times, are becoming cold and unspiritual. Successors are taking the places of those famed for their spiritual ministry, who unsettle faith, and alarm by throwing doubt upon truths received as such in every past age of the Church. Great is truth, and it must and will prevail. But, in the meantime, what confusion may arise, and how may the people be left as sheep without shepherds! It is surely necessary that in all the Churches a stand should be made by those who believe in the eternal verities, and whose faith remains unshaken in the Old Testament and the New. Truth must always suffer by being associated with that which is false and perilous.

There is another aspect of this question, as to the truth and authority of the Old and New Testaments, which is of great importance. Simultaneously with the progress of unbelief, there has been a rapid progress of superstition, a great advance, not only, nor even so much, of Roman Catholicism as of Romish doctrine. Has this simultaneous progress been accidental? We are certain that it has not. In reading the 'Apologia pro Vitâ suâ' of the late Cardinal Newman, we can easily see that scepticism, and especially doubt, as to authority of Scripture, led him gradually to the Church of Rome. He had eminently a religious mind, and he could not remain in the desert region of unbelief. He sought for a solid, intelligent foundation for his belief. He was influenced by those doubts so prevalent at Oxford, as elsewhere. So he fled at last to the Church of Rome, which solves all doubts by declaring its infallibility, and which professes to make the Scriptures secure as the word of God, by the authority of the Church. Thus Cardinal Newman not merely got an authority, but he had his faith secured in the Scriptures which he loved. The same influences are acting, consciously or unconsciously, on many minds of less power than that of Cardinal Newman. Many persons cannot bear to be without a secure faith. They are alarmed by the doubts thrown on the Divine authority of the Scriptures. They are told that the word of God is in the Scriptures, but that the Scriptures throughout are not the word of God. They must find out the truth, therefore, for themselves as they best can, having no authority any longer. But how can they do so? Here is one passage or narrative they have built on, but they are suddenly informed by some friend, or from the pulpit, that it is not trustworthy—that it is a forgery or invention. What are they to do? Are they to make a religion for themselves, by finding out certain passages that suit them, and supposing these to be the word of God? It is not a satisfactory process. Instead of growing in faith, they find themselves daily losing faith. It appears as if soon nothing would be left. In despair they rush to authority—first, perhaps, to the authority generally of the Church. But, then, what is the Church? Which section possesses the authority? There is confusion. So at last they look to that section which, at all events, existed before the Reformation, and which professes to be infallible, with an infallible living representative on earth. They accept its claims. Their doubts and restlessness disappear. They can now receive even the Bible with confidence, because the infallible Church has declared it to be the word of God. Thus, by a very simple process, which can easily be discerned, the false criticism of the Scriptures, based on a foregone infidelity, leads to haziness and uncertainty, from which refuge is at last sought in the Church of Rome. If we cannot accept the principles of the Reformation, which centred all authority in the word of God, then we must either have no religion, or flee to the refuge of some authority which professes to be infallible, and to give its imprimatur to the Scriptures—and such authority the Church of Rome claims. The going over to that Church of not a few earnest minds, and the rapid growth of a religion which centres in Church authority, in barren ecclesiasticism, even apart from the Church of Rome, are principally due to attempts, through the channel of a professed criticism — which takes for granted infidel principles as its basis—to destroy belief in the statements of both the Old Testament and the New. The more that these attempts succeed in deceiving men, and causelessly shaking their faith in the word of God, the more rapid will be the progress of Romanism. The Church of Rome is not strongly opposed to the pseudo-criticism. It rather favours it. It knows well how greatly it strengthens its own claims, by leading men to flee to it to find security even for their belief in the Scriptures. This false criticism is thus playing into the hands of the Church of Rome, and, if not checked, there will probably be a very large accession to that Church in England, Scotland, and America. It is among these Anglo-Saxon nations, where there is much religious life, as well as great commercial prosperity, that Rome is now putting forth her strongest efforts; and nothing helps her so effectively as doubts of the Divine authority and inspiration of the Old and New Testament Scriptures.

Yet many are playing with this question, and actually treating it as of little importance; and many, even good, earnest people, who do not understand it, are looking on—thinking most blindly that it does not much affect them, so long as it leaves them a crucified and risen Saviour. How long will it do so?

There could not be a greater delusion than to treat lightly the question of inspiration. It is of vital moment. Those who tamper with the Old Testament, and treat many of its statements as of little importance, are fostering unbelief. They may and do often themselves cling to the great principles of the faith, but the logical result, in no long period—in the minds, certainly, of their children—will be the rejection of Christianity as a God-given religion. The Old Testament was regarded by Jesus Himself and the Apostles as of absolute Divine authority, and they rested on it the claims of the Messiahship. The Christian idea, as impressed by our Lord and His Apostles, was that from the time of the fall there was preparation for the work of redemption; that God revealed Himself to man, and that this revelation was, so far as necessary, written down afterwards by men, inspired of the Spirit. It was God's message, and not man's message, though men's faculties were employed in the giving of it, so that it was both human and

Divine. The Spirit acted not on them as dull instruments, but as living men, breathed on them and prepared them to write those things which they did, according to their special circumstances and idiosyncrasies—but still inspired of the Holy Ghost. The Scripture points towards the Messiah from the beginning. It introduces us to the family of Abraham, chosen of God; created, we may say, of God— for as yet Abraham had no child—for the purpose of preserving light in the earth, and especially of preparing the way for the promised Messiah. It describes to us the preparation for the occupation of Palestine by the children of Abraham, then the deliverance from Egypt by the mighty hand of God, then the forming of them into a nation under the guidance of Moses, specially directed by God. It points forward through the sacrifices, and especially that of the Paschal Lamb—but through all—to the sacrifice to be made for sin on the cross. It pictures David a king anointed of God to symbolize the great King that was to come to rule over the nations—the son, and yet the Lord of David. It gives us the inspired Psalms suitable to the Church, Jew and Gentile, to the end of time, the most wondrous songs of praise and thanksgiving, and of adoration, and confession, of conflict with evil, and triumphing of good, where every phase of feeling of the renewed heart in its relations to God is not merely described, but is uttered with clearness and power— written therefore evidently for all times and all peoples, and yet, notwithstanding the representations of the critics, we believe chiefly by *one* man, whose voice sounds clearly through the most, if not all, of those ascribed to him. Many of these Psalms, in the most unmistakable method, make reference to the great Messiah whom the Jews expected, and to whom they applied them, *before* He came. The Old Testament contains the prophecies which in the sublimest pictures represent the mission of the expected King, the blessings that were to flow forth to Jew and Gentile under His reign; the new spiritual life that was to appear in the world, breaking down fiercest passions and converting swords into ploughshares, and spears into pruning-hooks, and filling the earth with peace and gladness, instead of with warfare and misery. These prophecies are full of the Messiah; they announce, as with trumpet sound, the advent of the great King. They become clearer and clearer as the ages advance and the hope brightens. It is impossible to read the Old Testament with intelligent thought without seeing the approach of a great Deliverer to purify and rescue the earth from slavery and bondage. It gives in the much-maligned Book of Daniel, the power of which the unbelieving critics are determined to destroy, its descriptions of great earthly kingdoms, and in the midst of them the little stone, cut out without hands, which grew to be a great mountain and filled the whole earth.

In this Book of Daniel there is all the statesmanlike grasp of one accustomed to direct the affairs of empires. It bears the strongest internal evidence of the authorship of one so placed as Daniel is represented to have been. Its object is to show, as the other prophets signified, but this with more distinctness as to the method, that God rules the kingdoms of the world, and that all the events from the beginning to the end are subordinate to the ushering in of that kingdom which shall fill the whole earth. Daniel is very clear in its statement as to the Messiah and His kingdom, and gives also distinct indications as to the time of His appearing. Thus all through the Old Testament, from the beginning to the close, there is the sound of the tread of the great Deliverer—the preparation for His coming. There are not merely prophecies here and there, but there is a prophecy throughout—in the selection of Abraham, in the promise given to him as to all nations being blessed through him, in the declarations of Moses as to the future of the people, and the coming of the great Prophet in the Psalms which speak much of Him, and are fitted to celebrate His praises in every age of the Church, in the prophecies of Isaiah and of all the prophets, both before the exile and after.

CONCLUSION.

JESUS CHRIST is the Light of all the ages, the Centre of all history. Expectations were aroused during many ages before He appeared. There are indications of this in the traditions of a number of nations. At last He appeared in the world as a man of humble position—a man of sorrows—not assuming the kingly power as the Jews expected that their Messiah would do, but going about from village to village healing the diseases of the people and speaking glad tidings to the outcast and sorrowful; bitterly opposed and denounced by the ecclesiastics of the day, because He condemned their hypocrisy and would not acknowledge their claims; at length put to death by a criminal sentence after He had been excommunicated amidst the execrations of the most influential and learned doctors of the Jewish Church. So far from assuming earthly kingly power, as was expected of the Messiah, and leading forth Israel to conquest and vast empire, His mission was apparently closed amidst defeat, and clouds, and darkness. Nothing seemed more unlikely, humanly speaking, than that His name should continue to be known in the earth. Yet, speaking to a little company of men of no influence, He claimed the highest power and announced the final universal triumph of His cause. Many have made high claims and pretensions, but their names have passed away, unknown and forgotten, in a few years, or been held up to ridicule. But Jesus, the despised, the excommunicated, put to an ignominious death as a criminal, has had His claims *verified by history*. He walked in humble guise, the Son of the Eternal King. The name of the despised Nazarene, whom the Jews thought that they had destroyed, began to be known, far and wide, from the Day of Pentecost. That name has risen above every name. Thus the prophets were vindicated. The humble Jesus was proved to be mightier far than all the kings of earth. He gave evidences of His heavenly glory and of His kingly power when, according to the promise, He sent down the Holy Spirit to dwell in the hearts of His followers. He won the hearts of multitudes to Himself through the preaching of the Gospel, so that men became His willing, loving subjects, and many thought nothing of sacrificing their property and giving their lives for Him. The ages have rolled on. Christianity, which began with triumphs among men of all countries and positions, so that the name of Jesus was known far and wide in the Roman Empire, has continued to hold its position ever since amidst storms and conflicts. The Churches have passed through perils and darkness, but the name of Jesus has not been forgotten. The light has arisen again and again after the darkness. And what has been the instrument used for this purpose? Surely the *Scriptures of the Old and New Testament*. It was by means of them that many of the struggling, scattered Churches maintained the purity of the faith in ages of much darkness and ignorance, as when the wandering pedlars of the Waldenses committed the Scriptures to memory, and spread the knowledge of them through many a country which they visited with their wares. It was by means of them that Wycliff gave forth the clear sound of the Gospel to England and other lands at the close of the fourteenth century. It was by the reading of them, under strong mental conflict, that Luther raised his trumpet voice against the heathen corruptions of the Papacy, and that the Reformers brought back many in all countries to Christianity, as first proclaimed by Jesus and His Apostles. It was through diligent study of them, under the guidance of the Spirit, that, when Protestantism had become cold and formal, the great evangelists of last century roused England and Scotland and America from their slumbers, and created that great missionary enterprise which has been the glory and the blessing of the century. The name of Jesus has been honoured, age after age; it has been recovered from the superstitions and corruptions in which men have often sought to bury it, by the testimony of the Scriptures. What great spiritual revival has ever taken place apart from the earnest, reverent study of the Scriptures, both of the Old and New Testaments, as throughout the Word of God? These Scriptures were intended to bear witness to Him, as the Light of the world, from the beginning to the end. They foretold, by many methods, as devout men have clearly seen, His appearing in the world. Then when He did come, they gave the narratives of His sayings and deeds, and the doctrines connected with His death, and resurrection, and glory, and coming again. Jesus is, and has been, in all history. His name is far exalted above every name. But it is through the Scriptures of the Old and New Testaments, brought home indeed by the Spirit, that we know and understand Him. It is as we study the Scriptures that Christ stands out to our view in the fulness of His redeeming love, that we have the security of life eternal. If we rest upon these Scriptures as the Word of God, as everywhere of authority, then we grow in the knowledge of God, and are built up in the faith; but if we throw doubt upon their authority, and are left struggling with our feeble lights, to find out what is of God and what not, if we have no certain guide, the foundations are shaken. The great final effort of evil now is to throw down our stronghold. The attacks are now directed chiefly against the Old Testament. Many have been carried away. But the Old Testament is a part of the living organism. It has not been shaken by genuine investigation, but only apparently shaken by those who apply to it the test of the anti-supernatural, and attempt to explain it as containing neither miracle, nor prophecy, nor God.

APPENDIX A.

THE POET BURNS.*

BY A HIGHER CRITIC OF A FUTURE CENTURY.

We have lately come across a valuable work of Professor Scharfschütze, well known as an able critic, on the works of the so-called poet Burns, whom, however, the Professor now proves to have never existed. The field of higher Scriptural criticism has long been exhausted. The many ingenious theories in regard to the origin of the Old and New Testament books, one after another, gave way. It is many years, almost generations, since the doubts cast upon the authorship and times of writing of different books were finally disposed of. Our readers can scarcely imagine the excitement of the controversy of the time. Many critics were for a long period engaged in the work. Ingenious theories were devised. But these theories generally contradicted each other. Gradually there was a retreat along the whole line. The testimony, strengthened by the then recent discoveries of the stone records recovered from buried cities, and by the generally more intimate knowledge of

* An article written by me, published in the *Christian Church*, some years ago.

the different countries at the periods referred to, became irresistible. The critics were thus driven from a very inviting field, though perilous to the peace of Christendom. The power of Christianity, which they thought they had shaken, is now immensely greater than it was at that period.

But there is still, happily, work for able critics, in other directions, of a more harmless kind. And no one of the present day has exhibited more acuteness than the learned Professor, whose work we are now considering. In this book he enters with much ability upon an interesting inquiry, and in our view establishes conclusively his various positions.

The first question is, Did ever such a man as this Burns exist? The Professor is prepared to allow that there may have been an individual of that name, who had, perhaps, a good deal to do with the collecting together and final editorship of the poems. As to his having himself written these poems, as alleged, or any at least but a very small part of them, all scholars are now agreed that the idea must be given up. The Professor recognises at least five different writers. These five, at all events, he has distinctly proved, as we shall now show by a brief reference to the evidence given.

In the first place we have the great division, at once apparent, from language itself. These poems are in two very distinct dialects—we might say languages. The most of them are in what he calls old Doric Scottish—the finest specimens that we have of that language, with its touching beauty and tenderness, in which it surpasses the contemporary English. They contain a number of masterpieces in this dialect of, however, very different kinds. The Professor has given various specimens of each in his volume. When these are placed in juxtaposition, it is easily seen that they proceed from different sources. Some are national songs, very many are love-songs, others are descriptions of nature. There is thus a great variety, indicating different writers, and the Professor believes that the Scotch poems are a selection of the poems current at the period at which the editor lived, and, say, during the two previous centuries. Some few of them are, perhaps, even considerably older, though the language may have been slightly changed by the editor so as to make them understood at the time. The following, for instance, must have been written at a period much earlier than that to which it is ascribed. At the close of the eighteenth century Scotland had been long united to England, and there were no longer feuds between the two countries, whereas this poem breathes the spirit of national hate, and also of the slave longing to be free. We quote from the noble war-song, ' Scots wha hae wi' Wallace bled,' perhaps sung on many a bloody battle-field :

> ' By Oppression's woes and pains !
> By your sons in servile chains !
> We will drain our dearest veins,
> But they shall be free !
>
> ' Lay the proud usurpers low !
> Tyrants fall in every foe !
> Liberty's in every blow !—
> Let us do or die.'

This was evidently written at a time when Scotland was much oppressed by England. We seem to hear the very clanking of the chains. The probability is that it is a song of a very early period—the thirteenth or fourteenth century—adapted and somewhat modernized by the editor.

But to look again to the different kinds of poetry, there are these patriotic songs. Then there are a large number of love-songs. Even these are of very varied types, and indicate different authors. Then there are poems descriptive of objects of external nature and scenery. The Professor has proved his position beyond all doubt to men of scholarly mind, that these poems in what he calls the Doric Scottish dialect are a collection written by men of different periods, and with different sympathies. Possibly they may even have grown up by frequent verbal repetition into many of the beautiful forms which they assumed before they were finally adjusted.

But, again, there is another most clear division. There are a number of the poems, classified under the name of Burns, in the pure English of that day, quite a different language—more stately, but less winning. The style of these poems is also different, in harmony with the different genius of the language. Take, for instance, the following:

> ' Edina ! Scotia's darling rest !
> All hail thy palaces and towers,
> Where once beneath a monarch's feet
> Sat Legislation's sovereign powers !
> From marking wildly scattered flowers,
> As on the banks of Ayr I stray'd,
> And singing lone the lingering hours,
> I sheltered in thy honoured shade.
>
> ' Here wealth still swells the golden tide
> As busy Trade his labour plies ;
> There Architecture's noble pride
> Bids elegance and splendour rise ;
> Here Justice from her native skies,
> High wields her balance and her rod ;
> There Learning, with her eagle eyes
> Seeks Science in her coy abode.'

How entirely different the stately and somewhat stiff measure of this poem from that of the tender Scottish songs! One man could not have possibly written both—and that one man, represented as scarcely above an uneducated peasant, could in no case have written English of such purity.

But the Professor directs attention, also, to internal differences of a moral and religious kind. In Burns' poems there is a beautiful picture of the life of a godly peasant, evidently written by one who had the deepest sympathy with the religion of his country. This beautiful poem, after describing the pious home of a cotter and his earnest family prayer, says:

> 'From scenes like these Old Scotia's grandeur springs,
> That makes her loved at home, revered abroad:
> Princes and lords are but the breath of kings,
> An honest man's the noblest work of God.'

The man that wrote this poem must have been an enthusiast for his country's religion. All men of intelligence will, of course, see that the same writer could not possibly have written another poem called 'The Holy Fair,' in which pictures are given of Scotch religion by no means flattering, and evidently with keen enjoyment of the descriptions given. There is a most extraordinary mixture in these poems in this respect. There are a few, besides the 'Cotter's Saturday Night,' that show a great sympathy with earnest religion; there are a number of others, including even addresses to the devil, that are really profane. And so in regard to their moral character. Some are pure and elevated; many are the very opposite. Some of the finest poems, as poems, as 'Should Auld Acquaintance be Forgot,' are drinking songs, and drinking was the great vice of Scotland at that period.

Then, again, there are poems which exhibit the most tender and sensitive sympathy with Nature, evidently the work of another hand. There are the 'Mouse' and the 'Daisy,' familiar to all readers of poetry. What could be more touching than the description of 'A Winter's Night,' or more tender than the following verses of it?—

> 'Listening, the doors and winnocks rattle,
> I thought me on the ourie cattle,
> Or silly sheep, wha bide this battle
>   O' winter war,
> And through the drift, deep-lairing, sprattle,
>   Beneath a scaur.
>
> 'Ilk happing bird, wee helpless thing,
> That in the merry months of spring
> Delighted me to hear thee sing,
>   What comes o' thee?
> Where wilt thou cower thy chittering wing,
>   And close thy e'e?'

Here, then, there is another vein of poetry, of a most exquisitive kind.

We must bring this matter quickly to a close. The conclusions of the learned Professor, the grounds of which he has stated with great fulness, may thus be summarized: The Burns poems are as poetry a most beautiful collection or selection, maintaining far too high a level throughout to have been the production of one man. They also belong to different periods and different types of character and thought. The opposing elements are most striking.

He is able to predicate with certainty at least five different hands as traceable in them. The poems in the English and Scotch dialects, so exceedingly different in language as well as thought, are by men of different countries; and the Scotch have perhaps just been a little too grasping in claiming these beautiful English poems for one of themselves. Then, again, the ballad poems, as 'Scots wha hae wi' Wallace bled,' belong evidently to a much earlier period, when Scotland was at bitter feud with England. This divides the Scottish poems into two parts. But they must be apportioned still further to different authors. There are evidently two writers of entirely opposite moral and religious convictions. This may be seen even by the most cursory readers. Here, then, we have at least three writers of the Scotch poems:—1. The writer of the older part, when Scotland and England were bitter foes. 2. The enthusiastic admirer of the Scottish religion of a later period. 3. The keen and sarcastic foe of that religion.

One author of the English poems and these three of the Scotch make at least four different writers. But the poems descriptive of natural scenery, evidently by another hand, supply a fifth. The five are thus clearly proved; but the Professor thinks that many of the poems may have been only adapted by one of the five. They probably existed in five different books, each of which may have been in great part original. But in the end they were put together, in a curious mixed fashion, as if to hide their varied origins, by some editor—who may have possibly been called Burns, probably a man of extensive reading, but not much literary faculty, or he would have arranged them in a better fashion. The poems are beautiful, but the arrangement is extraordinary. This editor was probably a keen Scottish patriot, and, with an excusable wish to ring the fame of some great name for his country's glory, he attributed all these poems to one man. However the mistake happened, happen it did, as now proved most clearly to the satisfaction of all scholars. It is, in fact, ascertained knowledge.

There was no such poet as Burns. Many may be startled by this discovery. Some, no doubt, will insist on the importance of the historic testimony to the existence of the man and to the authenticity of his reputed works. They will insist on the general and undisputed belief that they were his, till a recent period. But such evidences fade into insignificance when seen in the light of that searching, careful, learned inquiry, on internal grounds, pursued in the volume which we have noticed. Let our doubtful capable readers read the book for themselves, and all their doubts must vanish.

The reasons here are much stronger than those of the 'higher critics,' in regard to Daniel or any of the other books—apart from the denial of the miracles and prophecy. Let our readers try the system with other known authors.

APPENDIX B.

THE MIRACLES OF THE TALMUD AND OF THE SPURIOUS GOSPELS, ETC.

IT is interesting to note the way in which Jews and Christians dealt with miracles when they invented them, and what kind of Bible we should have had, if the rationalistic view of the origin of the accounts of the miracles were correct! How does the contrast impress both the truthfulness and the Divine guidance or inspiration of the Scriptures!

To illustrate the 107th Psalm—'They that go down to the sea in ships, that do business in great waters, these see the works of the Lord, and His wonders in the deep'— Rabbi Bar Chuna says that he once saw a bird so tall that its head reached to the sky, and its legs to the bottom of the ocean. The water in which it stood was so deep that a carpenter's axe which had fallen in seven years before had not then reached the bottom. He also saw a frog as large as a village containing sixty houses. This frog was swallowed up by a serpent, and this serpent in turn by a crow. The crow flew and perched on a cedar, and this cedar was as broad as sixteen waggons abreast. There is also an account of a fish which was killed by a worm. This fish, when driven ashore, destroyed sixty cities, and sixty cities ate of it, and sixty cities salted it, and with its bones the ruined cities were rebuilt. Stories are also told of fishes with eyes like the moon, and of horned fishes 300 miles in length. To illustrate Amos iii. 8, a story is told of a lion which one of the Cæsars wished to see. At 400 miles' distance he roared, and the walls of Rome fell; at 300 miles he roared again, and all the people fell on their backs, and Cæsar fell on his throne. Cæsar then prayed for his removal to a safer distance. It is also said that a young unicorn one day old is as large as Mount Tabor, and that Noah, not being able to get one into the ark, bound it by its horn to the side. An account is given of the river Sanbation, which flows with stones all the six days of the week, but rests on the Sabbath day. A miracle is described of one rabbi killing another rabbi in a drunken fit, and then working a miracle which restored him to life. In the following year he again invited the rabbi to drink with him, but he declined on the ground that miracles are not wrought every day. It is said that the men of the Messianic period will be 200 ells high. The land of Israel will produce cakes, and cloths of the finest wool. The wheat will grow on Lebanon as high as palm-trees, and a wind will be sent by God to reduce it to fine flour for the support of those who gather it. Each kidney (of wheat, Deut. xxxii. 14) will be as large as the kidneys of the fattest oxen. In every cluster of grapes there will be thirty jars of wine. Jerusalem will be built three miles high; the gates of the city will be made of pearls and precious stones thirty ells high and thirty ells broad.

In the spurious narratives of the post-Apostolic period, the following are specimens of stories of Jesus' childhood. At His birth all kinds of motion suddenly ceased. Birds stopped in the midst of their flight; men at table with their hands to their mouths were unable to eat. When a child, He turns some children who refuse to play with Him into kids. A child by accident runs against Him, He says, 'Thou shalt fall and not rise,' and the child dies on the spot. His master strikes Him; Jesus curses him, and he dies. A favourite amusement of His was to make beasts and birds of clay in the presence of companions, and then to animate them and to make them run or fly away. As to His later years, it is said that He appeared to His disciples sometimes as a youth, sometimes as an old man, sometimes as a child, sometimes larger, sometimes less, sometimes so tall as to reach to the heavens. There is a description of the military standards making of themselves an obeisance to Him when He was brought before Pilate. There is also a story of a picture of Him, presented to Gamaliel by Nicodemus, which, when pierced by the Jews, gave forth blood and water. We are told that at the age of eight years, Joseph being anxious about a piece of work to be done, not having the right wood to do it, Jesus made a short piece of wood of the same length as a longer one. In another book we have accounts of a long conference between Nero and Simon Magus and the Apostles Peter and Paul, in which the greatest nonsense is talked, and which ends by Simon's making a flight to heaven, Paul looking up full of tears at seeing Simon's success, and adjuring Peter to interpose, and Peter's looking steadfastly towards Simon and saying: 'I adjure you, ye angels of Satan, who are carrying him into the air to deceive the hearts of the unbelievers, by the God that created all things, and by Jesus Christ, whom on the third day He raised from the dead, no longer from this hour to keep him up, but to let him go.' And immediately, being let go, he fell into a place called Sacra Via—that is, Holy Way—and was divided into four parts, having perished by an evil fate.

APPENDIX C.

THE NEGATIVE CRITICS AND THE PROPHETS.

THE Dean of Canterbury, Dr. Payne Smith, in his Bampton Lectures on 'Prophecy—a Preparation for Christ,' says, speaking of the German negative critics and Isaiah:

'Whenever these German critics get into a difficulty and do not know what to do with any portion of the prophetical books, they invent an ancient prophet or a modern prophet, or a great unknown or a little unknown, till one is weary of such commonplace makeshifts. Thus the last twenty-seven chapters (of Isaiah) are written by a "great unknown" who lived at Babylon at the end of the exile; but, first, he did not write the opening words, he borrowed them; he wrote, however, the controversy with idols and the account of the capture of Babylon; but when you reach the very kernel of the book—chapter fifty-three—Ewald owns that it could not have been written at Babylon. He even thinks that it may describe Isaiah's own martyrdom; or, if not, then the martyrdom of someone else, but at all events the sorrows spoken of were suffered under Manasseh. Why? Simply because the prophecy would have been almost more remarkable in the mouth of an exile of Babylon than in that of Isaiah. To get rid of the Messianic character you must affirm that it is historical, an account of some past tragedy. Tradition says that Isaiah was sawn asunder: it is certain that Manasseh was a tyrant; ergo, by the higher criticism logic, it was Isaiah who bore our griefs and carried our sorrows. Well then come chapters fifty-sixth, from the ninth verse, and fifty-seventh. It is a passage which has brought great ridicule upon the negative critics. No rational men could believe that it was written at Babylon, as they at first innocently affirmed. But Ewald is equal to the emergency. It was copied from an "ancient prophet," and must be printed in italics But chapters fifty-eight and fifty-nine are almost as unmanageable; so they, too, must be printed in italics, and assigned to a "modern prophet," an imitator of Ezekiel. And now there are no great difficulties till chapter sixty-three. Judah had nothing to fear from Edom and Bosra at Babylon. And so the first six verses are printed in italics again, and the passage is borrowed from the prophet who wrote chapter fifty-eight. And all the rest Ewald fairly gives up. "The great unknown" may have written it, but at a later time and under different historic circumstances. Chapter sixty-six, verse six, which shows that the temple was still standing when the prophecy was composed, refers to a time, he says, subsequent to the decree of Cyrus, and the weak commencement of the rebuilding of the Holy City. Observe then, omitting the opening words, eleven chapters out of twenty-seven—that is, all the crucial passages—are confessedly irreconcilable with the theory of "a great unknown" having written this magnificent composition at Babylon. Either, then, this book was written by Isaiah, as the Jews constantly affirm from the most ancient times, or it is a piece of patchwork. The mental calibre of the man who can believe it to be the latter must be infinitely small. The theory of a Babylonian Isaiah is dead.'

Speaking generally of alleged interpolations in the prophets, he says :

'Never were there writers whose style is more exactly marked than the prophets, and the idea that large interpolations are possible, and that you may pull a prophecy to pieces and divide its dismembered limbs among a heap of other writers, simply means that people know so little of the subject that they suppose that Hebrew literature is unlike every other literature. If I were to affirm that Horace wrote considerable portions of Virgil's "Georgics," the assertion would be treated as ridiculous : not because it is more ridiculous than what has been said about Isaiah, for instance, but simply because men generally know enough of Latin to be able to form a judgment upon the subject. If a man makes a similar assertion as regards the writers of the Old Testament, he can always count upon the ignorance of his readers. They do not know that the prophets have each one his own marked and peculiar style.

THE END.

Elliot Stock, Paternoster Row, London.